Embracing Humanity

 Ministries

15 The Chambers, Vineyard
Abingdon OX14 3FE
+44 (0)1865 319700 | brf.org.uk

Bible Reading Fellowship (BRF) is a charity (233280)
and company limited by guarantee (301324),
registered in England and Wales

ISBN 978 1 80039 226 7
First published 2024
10 9 8 7 6 5 4 3 2 1 0
All rights reserved

Acknowledgements
Unless otherwise stated, scripture quotations are taken from the The New Revised
Standard Version Updated Edition. Copyright © 2021 National Council of Churches
of Christ in the United States of America. Used by permission. All rights reserved
worldwide. Quotations marked 'NRSV 1995' are taken from New Revised Standard
Version Bible: Anglicised Edition, copyright © 1989, 1995 the Division of Christian
Education of the National Council of the Churches of Christ in the United States of
America. Used by permission. All rights reserved.

A catalogue record for this book is available from the British Library

Printed by CPI Group (UK) Ltd, Croydon CR0 4YY

Embracing Humanity

A journey towards becoming flesh

Isabelle Hamley

BRF
Ministries

Contents

Foreword

Every year in Advent I find a greater sense of wonder at the idea of the Word made flesh. It just seems to be so extreme and risky. Babies are vulnerable, yet God becomes one. War zones are dangerous, especially for children, yet God chooses a war zone to be the place of his birth. Those in poverty have the highest rate of infant trauma, neonatal deaths and shortened lifespans. God is born into a poor family. Refugees combine the dangers of all the above, yet God is born in a place and time that creates enemies who force his family on to the road.

No sensible communications expert would say to the Word that this is how to get your message across. A baby in a manger sounds dramatic today, and centuries of more or less schmaltzy telling of the stories of Christmas have given us the impression that the world stopped its busy life and focused on a small and unimportant town called Bethlehem. But it did not. The Word became flesh, not with a shout of triumph but in a baby's whimper, unheard beyond a few feet. The Word lived in a small area and died with a cry unheard, again, beyond a few feet.

Yet now the world does more or less stop. As Isabelle Hamley writes about her childhood, even in an atheist family Christmas was an event; Christless certainly, but still an event, and not one called Yule or anything like that. The birth of Christ seems to stop the world in its most prosperous areas even more every year, in inverse proportion to the number of believers.

Isabelle has written a wonderful book of preparation for Christmas, a book to build excitement, open the eyes and relish the paradox of a God who loves us so much that he whispers his words of comfort and joy, heard only by those who listen. Her aim is to bring us face to face with Christ, to go through Advent travelling towards Bethlehem, and to find out who our travelling companions are. We know some. We travel with the shepherds, the short distance from dark hillside to awed wonder. We travel with the magi, the long and puzzled journey to a point of enlightenment and then flight. But most of all we travel with each other.

This strange journey to a point of hope that changes the world is not made with chosen companions – or rather, not with companions chosen by us. It is a journey with those very unlike us, in culture and experience, in belief and outlook, except that we are going the same way. In Isabelle's beautiful and thoughtful writing, the barriers we put up against those too 'other', too unlike us, are dissolved over the weeks of Advent, so that the end of journeying is a destination that draws us before the face of God translated into human understanding, and a journey in which we discover one another better.

Two changes come when Advent is travelled well. We change our understanding of God, and we change our understanding of what it is to be part of the church, that vast number who follow Jesus Christ, the baby in Bethlehem.

Justin Welby, Archbishop of Canterbury

Introduction

I grew up in a world without Christmas.

As a child in a virulently atheist family, going through the highly secular French education system, I simply did not hear the story of Christmas until I was a teenager. Of course, we had a tree and presents, and as an avid reader I came across rumours of Christmas in books, but nothing concrete or explicit. Christmas was just a cultural artefact, a time to get presents and endure distant relatives. Magic and wonder waned as soon as I stopped believing in Father Christmas (no mention of 'Santa' in my family, that would have been far too religious).

Watching my first nativity, age twelve, was a revelation. The sheer wonder of it still gives me goosebumps: the hard journey, the promise of a star, the extraordinary baby unrecognised while an indifferent world goes by. I still love nativities. In particular, I love school nativities. They're a wonderful, chaotic, odd take on the Christmas story. Sometimes they are so chaotic it is actually difficult to recognise much of the Christmas story in there, in between unicorns, aliens and robots. I love them, because they tug on a familiar story – after all, even in the weirdest, most outlandish interpretations, you still have Mary, Joseph and Jesus, and the wonder of the birth. At the same time, they bring in so much else – all the strange, quirky aspects of our humanity, with joy and celebration that we can't always explain, and the occasional bunfight between ox and donkey. School nativities are a cacophony of humanity. And this is the world, the people God has come to walk with, in their habits and cultures and choices, even the questionable ones.

Even when the message passes by those gathered, focused as they are on taking pictures of their own little cherubs dressed in makeshift donkey costumes, nevertheless, in this echo of the story, there is something of God-with-us, still often unrecognised, but present nonetheless. There is still something of God coming into the reality of our lives, right in the midst of them, and taking shape in the particularities of where we are. Christmas points us to who God is, but it also points us towards what it means to be human and how God chooses to become one of us.

The 21st century is a strange time to be human. Today rumours are not of God made flesh, but of artificial intelligence, which may make many humans redundant. God became flesh, but human beings seem constantly eager to escape being flesh: we make disincarnated, disembodied 'intelligence', in our image. We try to flee our bodies in virtual reality, and modern medicine gives us ways to change the bodies we do not like or want and prolong life far beyond previously natural ends. What can the Christmas story tell us about who we are in this changing world? What does it mean for the Good News to be good news for the whole human person, rather than just minds or souls? Who are we called to be, as we walk with the God who walks with us?

To be a Christian is to believe that God, the creator of the universe, is beyond anything we can imagine or fathom. Yet it is also to believe that this God, who created us, stooped to earth and chose to become one of us. It is to believe that in God's eyes, our humanity is not something to transcend, but something to embrace.

This Advent, I invite you on a journey to explore humanity in the light of Jesus' coming. Each day, we will explore a different aspect of Jesus' humanity, of God's wholehearted embrace of the world he created. Humanity is not an easy thing to live with; we often struggle with our limitations, and the realities of a physical world we cannot ever fully control, and a human world of interactions that brings as much pain as it brings joy. And yet this is the existence that God chose and embraced. God brought salvation not by removing us from our humanity, but by entering it and inviting us into a journey of transformation within it.

Dwelling on the person of Jesus is an invitation for all of us to befriend our humanity, explore God's call to follow in the footsteps of Jesus and learn to live life in all its fullness – the life of humanity reconciled to God, to one another and, perhaps hardest of all, to itself.

DAY 1

Prologue

The angel said to her, 'Do not be afraid, Mary, for you have found favour with God. And now, you will conceive in your womb and bear a son, and you will name him Jesus.'
LUKE 1:30–31

'Do not be afraid.' Four little words, and one of the most frequent commands given to human beings in the whole of scripture. The command always seems a little ironic: after all, God and angels only ever need to tell you to not be afraid when there is something frightening just round the corner! In the Bible the words 'do not be afraid' are, however, almost always accompanied by another set of words: 'For I am with you.' God tells us not to be afraid, not because there is nothing scary, nor because there is no danger or difficulty ahead, but because God is with us. God's presence overshadows and overcomes whatever it is that we may be afraid of.

In Luke, the story of God's journey towards embracing a human form begins with these words, 'Do not be afraid.' These are words that tell us much about being human: being human is a dangerous, risky business. Human beings are small creatures in an immense universe, subject to all kinds of forces, not least their own destructive impulses. But God says, 'Do not be afraid.' The angel's first greeting was, 'The Lord is with you!' So the presence of God is already assured. But something new is happening. After the familiar words 'do not be afraid' comes the usual refrain, in unfamiliar form. It is another assurance of the presence of God, but this time in strange, unexpected fashion: 'You will bear a son.' 'God is with you' now takes on a much more intimate, almost invasive meaning. God will be with Mary, and all humanity, in a completely different way. God is coming to 'be with' his creatures by sharing their humanity.

We often say that Jesus was fully human, and that therefore he experienced the whole range of human emotions. I wonder whether he was ever scared. I wonder what it would have been like, for the God of all immensity, the God who flung stars into space, in that instant, to be reduced to a newly implanted embryo – just a few cells, small, contained, unseeing, unhearing, completely dependent on the life-blood of another.

We often think of the incarnation as Jesus being born. But God came to be with humanity in Jesus nine months or so earlier, as a foetus slowly growing within Mary. Nine months of being confined, surrounded, enclosed within Mary's humanity. Nine months of waiting and growing into humanity. Nine dangerous months, and an even more dangerous birth – infant and mother mortality was high in the ancient world.

God made flesh was risky business – for mother and baby alike. 'Do not be afraid' was quite clearly the right greeting. But God is with us. God embraced humanity and did not take any shortcuts, however much easier it would have been!

The long wait before Christmas matters – God is present with his people, but hidden, barely noticed and dismissed. Mary probably wouldn't have been believed; her pregnancy wouldn't have been noticed for a while, and once it was, villagers around her would not have discerned the presence of God. They would have seen a teenage girl, pregnant out of wedlock. The first person we are told who noticed the presence of God was another baby: John the Baptist leapt in Elizabeth's womb in recognition (Luke 1:44).

Human beings aren't very good at recognising God. That's a consistent thread in the story – they look in palaces and high places, among luxury and ease, when God is hidden in faraway, irrelevant, humbler places. What do we fail to notice today? Where is God at work, this Advent time, around us?

If God wanted to embrace humanity, to self-reveal in ways humans could understand, why not come in a more obvious way? God comes softly and quietly, and enters the common life of humanity, the ordinary and routine. God embraces the reality that to be human is to be one of many, to live a life marked by what is ordinary, and makes it extraordinary.

These weeks of Advent are a time to befriend the ordinary and look for signs of God within it, not simply looking ahead to Christmas, as if all that matters is the destination we want to reach. The journey matters; the waiting is important, but not because waiting is a good thing in and of itself. Waiting matters because it prevents us from missing out on where God is at work *on the way*. And it is those signs of God already at work that prepare us to welcome Christmas Day in its glorious fullness and not look for God in the wrong places.

It is easy to overfocus on the end of the journey, the great event, to such a degree that our life is lived in the future, without attending to the present. When my daughter was little, we started a little tradition. We put up the empty crib in the lounge on Advent Sunday, and then dispersed all the different actors of the nativity around the house. Shepherds and sheep in a field faraway (but near a window so they could see the angels come!); the wise men furthest away from the crib, on a long journey; Mary and Joseph waiting in Nazareth in the dining room; a star suspended from the highest place over the stairs. Every day, we moved the characters a little nearer the crib. We told stories of what the wise men saw on the way. We gathered lots of different sheep around the shepherds. We took Mary on a journey to see Elizabeth and back.

Ahead of Christmas, all these characters were already moving, listening, acting in ways that showed God at work in their lives and in the life of the world. Christmas was long in the making; it was not a one-day single event. The threads of humanity, in its wonderful diversity of cultures, backgrounds and people, were being gathered by God, brought together and knitted into the story of salvation. God-made-flesh, God-with-us, was already inviting all of humanity to come near, embracing the needs and hopes of the world, whispering softly, 'Do not be afraid, for I am with you.'

As you set out into Advent, you may want to commit yourself to noticing one way in which God is present within every day of the month ahead and write it down. What made you notice? Does a pattern emerge? How does it feel to consciously notice God at work?

Immanuel, God-with-us,
Help us, this Advent, to discern your presence
in strange and unexpected places.
May we see you in the face of the stranger.
May we see you in the face of those we love.
May we see you in the face of those who turn away from us.
May we see you waiting at the side of the road.
Help us make space in our lives and in our imaginations,
so that the wonder of your presence
would never cease to amaze us,
and as we see our humanity
reflected in your story,
help us learn from you
what it is to be fully human
and made in your image.
Amen.

1

The Word became flesh

And the Word became flesh and lived among us, and we have seen his glory, the glory as of a father's only son, full of grace and truth.

JOHN 1:14

To be a Christian is to believe in God, who is beyond anything we can imagine, and yet also believe that this God, who created us, stooped to earth and chose to become flesh. 'Flesh' is a thick kind of word. It evokes something solid, real, something we can't ignore. It makes us look at bodies and how we think about and treat them. We don't often put 'flesh' and 'glory' in the same sentence, and yet this is what John does in the opening to his gospel. How do we understand this paradox, that flesh is so fragile and limited and yet can be the vehicle for God to reveal God's glory?

DAY 2

Embodied

He was in the world, and the world came into being through him, yet the world did not know him. He came to what was his own, and his own people did not accept him. But to all who received him, who believed in his name, he gave power to become children of God, who were born, not of blood or of the will of the flesh or of the will of man, but of God. And the Word became flesh and lived among us, and we have seen his glory, the glory as of a father's only son, full of grace and truth.
JOHN 1:10–14

'The Word became flesh.' How easy it is to read those words, on Christmas Eve or Christmas Day, and forget to stop for the wonder of it. The Word became *flesh*. 'Flesh' is such a practical, grounded word. Not just 'body', not just 'human', but 'flesh'. The Oxford English Dictionary defines flesh as 'the soft substance consisting of muscle and fat that is found between the skin and bones of a human or an animal'. The word 'flesh' is precise, unemotional and down-to-earth. The Word, a concept, an idea, a possibility, now becomes solid, in the way that animals and humans are solid, as an interconnected web of tissue and bones that somehow enables life as we know it.

The sheer physicality of Jesus is something that gospel writers pick up on repeatedly: Jesus gets hungry and tired; he needs to rest; he has dusty feet and needs to wash. To use the word 'flesh' leaves us nowhere to go but to accept the unimaginable: that human bodies are good enough, precious enough, for God to take shape within them, for concepts and ideas and ideals to be made real. This is quite extraordinary if we consider the history of the word 'flesh'. In much traditional discourse, flesh has had negative connotations. It has often been used to refer to bodily appetites and desires, usually in a negative way, opposed to the ways of the Spirit.

Scripture itself is more nuanced when it comes to talking about flesh. Flesh has a long history in the Bible. Right at the beginning, in Genesis 2, God takes out a rib and closes the human creature's flesh. And out of this flesh, another human being is made, which the first human recognises as 'bone of my bones and flesh of my flesh' (Genesis 2:23). From then on, every human being is born, made, of the flesh of another. This very early story affirms how interconnected human beings are, and 'flesh' symbolises the deeper bonds between them. This long line of connected material bodies stretches across centuries and generations, between the very beginning and the coming of the 'Word made flesh': the genealogy of Jesus traces the origins of this flesh both through human connectedness and through the word of God.

Flesh is the material of human existence, and within it lies both dust and glory, curse and blessing, the image of God and the reality of sin. It is within human bodies and bodily existence that both the power of sin and the power of the Spirit are at work, as Paul states in Romans 7. The stories of Old and New Testament speak of the ways in which human beings move away from the 'good' of their creation and seek ways of destruction: they abuse one another's bodies; they abuse creation around them; they organise their lives in ways that cause some to have more than they need, while others' bodies are left to starve. It is within these complex, embodied relationships that sin and brokenness take root.

But it is also where salvation comes and transforms. God works with his people to transform the way they live, the way they relate, the way they value one another and creation. The laws of the Old Testament, as well as the prophets, explore ways of living that care for justice, peace and prosperity. In the New Testament, the ministry of Jesus does not distinguish between body and soul; the Good News is good news for the whole person. Hungry, sick, despised bodies in the ministry of Jesus are seen, touched and restored to dignity. Bodies will be restored and transformed in the resurrection of the dead, too; bodies are not left behind for a better, more lofty reality. The resurrection that is promised is a *bodily* resurrection.

We often struggle with this concept. For a long time, western cultures have assumed a dualism, the idea that we have a body and a soul and that what really matters is the soul. But that could not be further from the picture of scripture. In Hebrew, you don't *have* a body; you *are* a body. To be human is to be this strange, complex mix of thoughts, feelings and flesh. The body is not something we can use for the sake of our 'real selves' or our inner sense of who we are, or that can be used by others independently of our sense of being. Our bodies are an intrinsic part of who we are, and what we do with them and to them matters for the whole person. This, then, is why so much of scripture is concerned with matters of justice, of social relationships and of greed, lust and violence – because the whole human person is affected.

And so, conversely, salvation is for the whole person. The sign of the promise at work, given to Abraham with circumcision, is a sign given in the body. Promises of renewal are clearly embodied: God promises to replace 'hearts of stone' with 'hearts of flesh' in Ezekiel 36:26, where flesh represents humanity as it should be: vibrant, faithful and loving. In Ezekiel 37, the image of sin works itself out in the 'valley of dry bones', where human beings lose their humanity entirely, but God acts in salvation by putting flesh back on bones. Later, the prophet Joel prophesies the coming of the Spirit 'on all flesh' (2:28).

In the New Testament, the word 'flesh' is sometimes used negatively. Paul, for example, talks of 'flesh' following its own desire as opposed to the spirit following Christ. But this is not about human beings as split in two between body and spirit; rather, it is a contrast between two ways of living, two ways of understanding – one rooted purely in what can be seen, in the material, and one rooted in relation to God and what cannot necessarily be seen. In these passages, 'flesh' represents a world that has separated itself from God, that has limited itself – that has reduced itself to flesh, rather than the whole person.

In contrast, salvation is symbolised by the bread of life, Jesus giving himself: 'The bread that I will give for the life of the world is my flesh… Unless you eat the flesh of the Son of Man and drink his blood, you have no life in you' (John 6:51, 53). Jesus' words are pretty stark, even disturbing! This is a deeply material, embodied picture of salvation. It is the Word made flesh that changes the story and renews the whole person. And when the person is transformed, we see salvation at work in their body just as we saw sin at work in their body: through transformed lives, not just through spiritual illumination.

Everything in the story of God says something that our culture somehow struggles to understand: bodies matter to God; bodies are not despised, they are precious; bodies are not just instruments to be used, moulded or exploited, they matter in and of themselves; bodies are not irrelevant, they are the place of salvation.

For reflection

- I wonder how you feel about being embodied. As Jim Cotter says, you are 'not a no-body, nor just any-body. You are some-body'.[1] What does this mean for you today, that your body, the whole of you, is precious to God?

- You may want to spend some time giving thanks for your body – for its amazing intricacy; for the way it connects you to other human beings; for the way in which it makes you, you.

- And you may want to bring before God all the things that you struggle with when it comes to being embodied.

God-made-flesh,
we often struggle with our bodies,
with pain, with tiredness, with hunger;
we struggle with what we see in the mirror;
we struggle with what we do and what is done to our bodies.
Help us hold our bodies
with the care and love that you took as you designed them,
fearfully and wonderfully made.
Help us cherish the body of others
and care for their well-being
with gentleness, generosity and justice.
In the name of Jesus, the Word made flesh.
Amen.

DAY 3

Related and dependent

Then the Lord God said, 'It is not good for the ground creature to be alone; I will make for him a helper to stand with him.'
GENESIS 2:18 (MY TRANSLATION)

For a few years I worked as a university chaplain. I once met a young woman who had come to the UK as the wife of an international student. She found life in England unbearably difficult. She was not allowed to work, and did not have the finances to study. Her English was not very good, and she found it hard to know where to go to make friends. The first time I visited her, she explained, 'I have never been alone in my life. I have six sisters and three brothers. I have never been alone. I always did things with my sisters, went out with them, I shared a bedroom with two of them. Until I came here, I didn't know what being lonely was.' In the UK, she was told that she was struggling with her mental health and needed therapy, that she had a problem being over-dependent. But I wondered, who is it who has a problem? Are human beings made to be alone? Or is it our society that is problematic, because there were so few places for her to connect, to meet others, to become part of a community? Why would it be wrong to feel lonely if you are, objectively, alone?

The early narratives of the book of Genesis explore what it means to be human. We often know them well – or think we do. They ask many existential questions with which we still struggle today: who are we? What are we? Where have we come from? Do we matter? Why are we here?

Genesis doesn't answer the questions through great philosophical or even theological musings; instead, scripture tells us a story about who we are. And the story says, 'You are not alone', and, 'You are part of something much bigger than yourself.' Genesis 2 is all about relationships. Human beings are made from the dust of the earth and the breath of God; they are indissolubly related to both God and the natural environment that is their home. Human beings are not independent, autonomous or self-made. They are connected, interdependent and need God, one another and the wider world.

How does this work? God takes a little bit of the ground, and creates a 'ground creature'. The writer here is playing with words. The word for ground, or earth, in Hebrew is *adamah*. The word used to describe the human being that has been made is '*ha-adam*' – the thing made out of earth, the groundling, the ground creature. 'Adam' is not yet a proper noun, or a name, but a description of this creature who is profoundly connected to its own environment. And yet it is a creature with a difference: it is animated by the breath of God. The ground creature is tethered to the ground, to earth, to the world, *and* is constantly animated by the reality of the presence of God. The creature is then placed in the garden it needs for its life to flourish. It is introduced to the many creatures around – and yet, the creature is lonely. Neither the natural world nor a relationship to the God of life is quite enough for the creature to flourish: they need another like them, a counterpart.

It is worth pausing here. I have sometimes heard Christians say, 'God is enough, or God should be enough', often aimed at me or friends when we were single and struggling. And yet, here, at the very beginning of scripture, we are told, 'It is not good for the ground creature to be alone.' Human beings need relationships – beyond God; they are made for relationships. I don't think that the passage is focusing on romantic relationships only. What the ground creature needs are partners, others to be with, a sense of belonging within a human community, people who will be different yet equal.

Therefore, God makes a helper. The word is often used elsewhere for God himself coming alongside human beings. It is a word of partnership. The helper is made 'to be opposite/in front/facing' (Genesis 2:20 in Hebrew – 'there was not a helper to be opposite/facing him'): the implication is of an equal relationship between partners and a generative relationship. It is together that the two human beings can go into the world, tend the garden, care for other creatures and give birth to human community.

At this point in the story, when the ground creature becomes two creatures, they become 'man' and 'woman' (the words are not used before): they find their identity in relationship. Interestingly, they are united by 'flesh': when the man says, 'flesh of my flesh', the underlying meaning in Hebrew is 'We are family; we belong together through an indissoluble link.' Their identity was first in relationship to the natural world (the ground – they are both *ha-adam*, ground creatures, human beings), and now their identity expands through being in relation with other humans. The Bible often speaks of human beings as belonging to 'all flesh' – an expression to speak of all living things. 'Flesh' connects human beings with one another and to the natural world.

The story does not stop there, of course. The big existential questions continue, and they ask not just why we are here, but also how we got in such a mess. Genesis 3 explores the answer through another story; this time it is a story of the search for independence. Until now, the two humans lived in symbiosis with their environment, with plants and animals, they walked with God in the garden, and with one another. They were interdependent. But when all goes wrong, they seek to move from being interdependent and related to being independent and autonomous. Instead of learning right and wrong in relation to God, they look to a tree and its fruit. The tree can give them knowledge to possess, to own, to keep for themselves, with no need to relate to or learn from another. They move away from depending on God to depending on themselves. As the consequences unfold, their relationship to one another breaks down, their connection to the natural world breaks down (in enmity with the serpent and the ground being hardened), and even their own sense of inner self and connection crumbles and they become ashamed of who they are, of their God-given bodies, and hide.

Independence is nowhere considered a virtue in this story or in the rest of scripture. And yet today, in the west, independence is usually seen as a moral and social good. We tell our children they must become independent adults. Western stories, films and economies often prize the 'self-made man' and the go-getting entrepreneur who seeks personal fortune or fame. We construct our world at the expense of the natural world. And we often speak of our identity as something only we ourselves can know, construct or choose.

But this is not the story of scripture. The story of scripture tells us not just that independence is not very good, but also that it is a lie: human beings are never independent. They are always dependent on one another, on their environment and on God. The question is whether they acknowledge it – and take responsibility for it. It is only when we recognise our interdependence that we can value the gifts and contributions of all within our communities: those who clean our streets, as much as doctors, as much as entertainers, as much as business executives. Without every part of the puzzle, our cities would break down, our food chain would fall apart and life could not be sustained. It is only together that we survive, in our complex society as much as in a simpler, agrarian subsistence economy. We have just become much better at hiding how much we depend on one another.

Scripture also constantly reminds us that we are ground creatures, interdependent with the natural world. The environmental catastrophe destroying our planet right now tells us this too. When human beings forget to tend the garden, to care for its creatures, to understand their place as *part of* the world, rather than *over* the world, they end up, like cartoon characters, sawing off the branch they are sitting on.

Finally, scripture tells us again and again that we are social beings. This is why Jesus keeps talking of 'the kingdom of God'. The picture of heaven is not one of endless individuals each relating to God independently; it is an image of community, of connection, of purposeful life together. Being social means that we are responsible for the shape of our life together. What I choose to do has an impact on other people. How I choose to be in the world, the things I do, the things I seek, the person I am, all have an impact on others around me and on the whole system. What's more, scripture tells us we are accountable for the impact we have.

Human beings are fickle creatures. We often think or portray dependence as weakness, even though all of us come into the world completely dependent on our parents and communities, and in declining years, most of us will again become dependent on others to care for us. And at many other points, in illness and trouble, we will need to depend on others. To be dependent is not to be weak, less adult or less human. Being dependent, needing others, is profoundly, deeply and beautifully human. It is an aspect of humanity that God himself embraces: in becoming a baby and needing breastmilk, care and protection from Mary and Joseph. Later, Jesus regularly accepted a dependent position: asking for water; asking for others to share their boat, their donkey, their upper room; and, towards the end, needing help to carry the cross. There is no shame or diminution of Jesus' humanity here, only a deep embrace of what it is to be part of the human race.

For reflection

- Have you ever felt tempted to hide your dependence on, or need for, other human beings? Why do you think that is?

- Who has shaped who you are and helps you be human today?

- Could you map out all the people who contribute to your life, paying particular attention to who may be hidden, and give thanks for them all?

God with us, child of the manger,
we thank you for those who have cared for us and will care for us;
we thank you for those who depend on us;
and we ask you to help us see
all those connected to us through the deep web of human
    existence.
Help us act responsibly, recognise our impact
and accept the help of others,
even as we seek to offer our own.
Amen.

DAY 4

Fragile and vulnerable

In spite of all this they still sinned;
  they did not believe in his wonders.
So he made their days vanish like a breath
  and their years in terror.
When he killed them, they searched for him;
  they repented and sought God earnestly.
They remembered that God was their rock,
  the Most High God their redeemer.
But they flattered him with their mouths;
  they lied to him with their tongues.
Their heart was not steadfast towards him;
  they were not true to his covenant.
Yet he, being compassionate,
  forgave their iniquity,
  and did not destroy them;
often he restrained his anger,
  and did not stir up all his wrath.
He remembered that they were but flesh,
  a wind that passes and does not come again.

PSALM 78:32–39

'Why are people so fragile?' This was my daughter's question at four years of age, faced with the serious illness of a family friend. Not 'Why is this happening to her?' or 'Why is there evil and death in the world?', as we grown-ups were asking. In her childlike way, she pointed to a truth that we often try to avoid. People are fragile, vulnerable. They break. And it is simply part of being human; an obvious truth to her.

Just as with independence, we human beings like to pretend we are more than we are – that we are strong, resourceful, resilient – and so we often treat breaking bodies and minds as shameful or something to hide. We often disregard the reality of our fragility and put one another at risk through reckless behaviour, conflict and war.

To be human is to be fragile and to risk hurt. The Old Testament speaks of fragility again and again, and the way in which it speaks of vulnerability is almost always embodied. The book of Job explores the utter vulnerability of human beings – before nature, before other human beings, in themselves, and before an inscrutable God. Job loses his family, his wealth and his health. His body is breaking under the strain, and his mind struggles to make sense of it all. He is overcome with grief and simply wants to erase his life – he 'cursed the day of his birth' (Job 3:1). Throughout the book of Job, 'flesh' is the place of affliction; it is flesh that wastes away, that bears the marks of vulnerability. Emotions are felt in the body. The writers of Job understood what we now call psychosomatic symptoms: what Job felt and experienced, he experienced in the whole of his person, with no false distinction between body and soul.

Flesh is what makes human beings weak and mortal. The people of the Bible – Job, the psalmists – are not shy about it. They draw attention to it, again and again. Human vulnerability means two things. First, one cannot trust 'in the flesh' but needs a bigger horizon for trust. It is only God who can be trusted for our ultimate safety. And second, human vulnerability means we have a responsibility to care for one another, because however vulnerable we may be, we are nevertheless precious in God's sight. These fragile creatures are made in the image of God.

The image of God therefore cannot be an image of invulnerability and strength. The image of God is seen in the very fragility, and at times weakness, of humanity. There is no human being who reflects the image of God any less for the fragility of their body or mind. God's image shines through whether we are sick or healthy, able-bodied or a person with disabilities, when we have mental health challenges, whether we are academically gifted or gifted at sports, whether we earn a living or not. God's image does not shine through *in spite of* our differences, but through them. It is only together, in our multiple strengths and vulnerabilities, that we can see different aspects of God in one another and learn to love God through loving one another.

The coming of God into the world does not start with an adult Jesus going round teaching and doing miracles. It starts with the incredible vulnerability of childbirth. Even today, childbirth is a risky business. Globally, 4.6% of children die before their 15th birthday. The most dangerous time is the month following birth, and 2.3 million babies die annually, according to the World Health Organization, with huge disparities between countries.[2] Archaeological data suggest that at the time of the birth of Jesus, infant mortality was as high as 50%. For God to come as a small human baby was a risky, vulnerable business. Even beyond the birth, he would have to be cared for and protected by a community. Political unrest added to the vulnerability of God made flesh, as Herod orders the massacre of children under two in an effort to erase the possibility of hope in a Messiah, and the young family is displaced and become refugees in Egypt. The story of God coming to earth mirrors the reality of our world, in its ugliness, fear and fragility. God made himself vulnerable, because he could not have become human, flesh, without it.

As Jesus becomes an adult, vulnerability does not recede. At the very beginning of Jesus' ministry, straight after his baptism, he is taken into the desert, a place of ultimate vulnerability – to hunger and thirst, to weather, to wild beasts and to all the things that humans may want to avoid to keep themselves safe, regardless of the cost. The temptation before Jesus in the desert is the temptation of safety, of invulnerability: a temptation to deny or transcend humanity. In face of this temptation, Jesus affirms that the answer to the fear of vulnerability is neither denial nor the pursuit of strength, but reliance on the promise of a God who loves us: 'One does not live by bread alone, but by every word that comes from the mouth of God' (Matthew 4:4). Christ suffers in vulnerability as the gospel story progresses: he is hungry, thirsty, tired. He grieves and weeps for the brokenness of the world. He is threatened with stoning and violence. His body is broken on the cross, and even in the resurrection still bears the marks of crucifixion. Vulnerability and brokenness – the scars – are taken right into the heart of God as Jesus goes to the Father.

The ultimate vulnerability of God, however, is located not in a vulnerable human body, but in a heart of love for God's creatures. It is God's love for humanity that brings him to be made flesh. It is God's love that brings Jesus to the cross. It is love and compassion that bring God to share our humanity, our vulnerability, and reach out in salvation.

In Christ, we see a model of how to respond to our fragility: in compassion and care. The psalmist expresses it beautifully: 'He remembered that they were but flesh, a wind that passes and does not come again' (Psalm 78:39). Our vulnerability prompts God to compassion: 'A bruised reed he will not break, and a dimly burning wick he will not quench; he will faithfully bring forth justice' (Isaiah 42:3); 'He will feed his flock like a shepherd; he will gather the lambs in his arms and carry them in his bosom and gently lead the mother sheep' (Isaiah 40:11).

Embracing our own vulnerability means we do not pretend: we do not pretend to be stronger or better; we do not pretend that some human beings are superior to others; we do not pretend to be okay when we are not okay. Embracing our vulnerability means we recognise who we are before God, recognise who other human beings are before God, and accept our responsibility to give and receive care, to accept and offer compassion.

True compassion goes hand-in-hand with vulnerability, because I can only be compassionate when I open my heart to love another and feel their pain, their brokenness, their struggle. Compassion demands that we do not flee from our shared vulnerability, but stare at it, stay within it and embrace it. It takes us deeper into vulnerability. And, together, we might then find ways of living better with the reality of who we are.

For reflection

- At what time in your life have you felt fragile or vulnerable? How has that made you feel?

- How do you respond to the fragility of others?

Loving God,
we thank you that your love
led you to put yourself on the line.
Help us love with the same willingness
without counting the cost.
Help us when we feel fragile
and afraid of breaking.
Bring others round us
to tend to our wounds
and care for our pain.
Help us recognise the vulnerability of others,
especially at times when we may feel strong.
Lord, teach us to love
as you yourself have loved us.
Amen.

DAY 5

Limited

Love never ends. But as for prophecies, they will come to an
end; as for tongues, they will cease; as for knowledge, it will
come to an end. For we know only in part, and we prophesy only
in part, but when the complete comes, the partial will come to
an end. When I was a child, I spoke like a child, I thought like
a child, I reasoned like a child. When I became an adult, I put
an end to childish ways. For now we see only a reflection, as
in a mirror, but then we will see face to face. Now I know only
in part; then I will know fully, even as I have been fully known.

1 CORINTHIANS 13:8–12

There is a myth at the core of many wealthy societies, a myth we often
teach our children, a myth that underlies Hollywood stories, reality TV
and many 'inspirational' school assemblies. The myth goes like this:
'You can be anything you want to be! You just have to work hard and
keep trying. Look at all these unlikely people who beat the odds and
got there!' This is not new – the fabled American dream also promised
rags-to-riches stories and the possibility of 'a land in which life should
be better and richer and fuller for everyone, with opportunity for each
according to ability or achievement'.[3]

On the one hand, it is a great storyline to help motivate children to
work, dream and hope, and to counter despair and the belief that our
life circumstances can never change. However, there is a dark side
to the belief that we can be anything we want to be. And this dark

side is: we cannot. Some people might achieve their goals, through ambition, luck, hard work and talent. But many will not, and this is not because they do not work hard enough or dream big enough. It is simply because human beings are all limited: we are limited by our bodies and minds, by our birth, by our chances in life, by what happens to us and is done to us, by external circumstances, and by the societies we live in and their biases.

The even darker side of pretending we can be whatever we want to be is that, if this is true, then those who struggle must struggle through their own fault. To believe that all of us can achieve anything takes away our collective responsibility to build a fair, just and compassionate society, where all of us seek the best possible life *together*.

Being limited is often seen as a negative today. Our world loves breaking limits – we celebrate explorers of the past, adventurers, those who go beyond the known frontiers of science; we develop medicine and push the human body beyond limits previously unknown. And yet, for all our efforts, human beings are still earthbound, fragile and mortal. Being limited is part of our humanness, the humanness that God created, loves and shared in Jesus. Jesus was a man (not a woman), Jewish (not Gentile), first century (not any other time), Middle Eastern (not African or European or American or Asian or any other ethnicity), of a certain height, weight and appearance. He was intensely particular and therefore, to a degree, limited to this particularity. And yet – Jesus represents *both* human particularity and God's reach to all.

As human beings, all of us are situated: we are part of one place and one time. We are born to one set of parents, raised within a certain culture (two or three overlapping ones sometimes), with one or two languages only as our mother tongue. Our bodies are particular and shape our social belonging – our sex, our ethnicity, our physical abilities. Combined, our bodies and stories shape our skills, interests and choices. None of us can claim to be the whole of humanity, to understand the whole of humanity. All of us are fully human, yet none of us are everything. We are flesh – and in the language of the Bible, we belong to 'all flesh', the whole of humanity. To be human is to belong to this wider horizon of human beings, who are both profoundly alike and profoundly unlike ourselves.

There are, of course, negative sides to being limited. Sometimes it may shatter dreams, when we realise we have neither the talent nor the opportunities to become the person we might have dreamt of being, or when life interrupts through illness, tragedy or other circumstances, and we are forced to change course. Wrestling with our limitations can be deeply painful. It brings us face-to-face with our lack of control of life and with the discrepancies between our dreams, our inner life, and reality. The challenge as a human person is to find a way to live well, making space both to face reality as it is and to keep up hope that things can be different – and recognise what can and should be challenged, changed and transformed, and what needs to be accepted and lived with. There is no manual, no easy way through this. The shape of the journey will be different for all of us and considerably easier for some than for others.

Two types of texts in the Bible speak to this. One is the stories that speak of the transformation of our desires: those stories where human beings learn to reshape how they see the world, where they learn from God and from one another how to live in healthier, better ways for themselves and their communities.

The story of the Hebrews in the desert, in Exodus, is this kind of story. They have come out of slavery, but do not yet know how to live free from the habits, economy and imagination of Egypt. It would be so easy for them to go somewhere new, and live as Egypt did: grasping, hoarding, competing for resources. Instead, they are led into the desert and learn to live off manna: every person gets their fill, every household has their needs met, and no one is allowed to take more than what they need, no one is allowed to hoard or compete. The people's imagination is being reshaped, so that they learn the difference between need and desire. What was limiting in Egypt was not resources, it was the human mind and human ways.

A different type of text would be the psalms of lament. In lament, the people cry out in the face of a world that restricts them in unfair, unjust and painful ways. They cry out against the ways in which sin affects human lives. But psalms of lament do not stop at crying out: they also call for God to act and bring transformation. The psalms of lament proclaim that some restrictions and limitations are not a natural aspect of being human, but a human-made consequence of sin and brokenness. And where this happens, it is challenged. The psalms of lament radically reimagine what the world could be like and dare to proclaim hope in a different future, even in the midst of despair.

Human beings find it difficult to know how to inhabit these stories. We often confuse what we desire for what we need, and we often justify unjust systems and actions because we seek our own fulfilment rather than working together, across our differences, for the common good. This points to another aspect of our limitations as human beings: we are often limited in our understanding of ourselves, of others and of God.

The apostle Paul speaks of this in 1 Corinthians 13:9–12: 'For we know only in part… for now we see only a reflection, as in a mirror, but then we will see face to face. Now I know only in part; then I will know fully, even as I have been fully known.' As people of 'flesh', we are often limited in our understanding of God and of the nature of life in God's eyes. This doesn't mean we can know nothing – but it does mean that we are limited and need some provisionality in the things we think we know and affirm. Paul is well aware of this, and in Corinth, where some were very certain of their gifts and words, he reminds them that they are limited and that, therefore, their overall guide should be love.

Love is what brings humans together, with one another and with God. It is the bond that enables us to transcend our limitations. The great mirage of believing we can be anything is to think that we can do it on our own, for ourselves. It is actually a huge limitation of the imagination, restricting our dreams and ambitions to the self. Human beings are not alone: they may be limited individually, but their limitations are a strength, not a weakness. It is because I am limited that I need another with me. It is because I am limited in my understanding of myself and the world that I need to make space for others to help me understand myself, understand them, understand the world and understand God. On my own I see very little. Together, we see much more. Our personal limitations as human beings call us to seek out others, so that together we can learn more of what it is to be human and see and hear more of God in the world, and, together, discern how to live well in the world God has created.

For reflection

- Think about all the things that are particular, unique about you. Maybe you could make a list, and spend some time praying through them. How do they make you feel? Are any of them 'limitations'? Are any of them opportunities? Spend time placing each of them before God, knowing that God holds each of these gently, carefully and preciously.

God of the entire universe,
who made yourself small, contained and earthbound for our
    sakes,
help us discover the sheer wonder of the things that make us who
    we are,
to rejoice in our differences
and learn to see them as an opportunity.
Help us make peace with what we need to accept
and fight for the things that need to change,
not simply for our sake,
but for the sake of all those we love,
and even those we don't.
In Jesus' name, Amen.

DAY 6

Mortal

When Mary came where Jesus was and saw him, she knelt
at his feet and said to him, 'Lord, if you had been here, my
brother would not have died.' When Jesus saw her weeping
and the Jews who came with her also weeping, he was greatly
disturbed in spirit and deeply moved. He said, 'Where have you
laid him?' They said to him, 'Lord, come and see.' Jesus began
to weep. So the Jews said, 'See how he loved him!' But some
of them said, 'Could not he who opened the eyes of the blind
man have kept this man from dying?'

Then Jesus, again greatly disturbed, came to the tomb. It
was a cave, and a stone was lying against it. Jesus said, 'Take
away the stone.' Martha, the sister of the dead man, said to
him, 'Lord, already there is a stench because he has been dead
for four days.'

JOHN 11:32–39

In 2020, the world came to a stop. To parody the words of a famous
prayer by Henry Newman (1801–90), the 'busy world' was 'hushed'
and 'the fever of life abated'. Suddenly, business and busyness halted,
and human beings were, largely, faced with themselves in lockdown
and faced with risk and danger when meeting others for the necessary
business of survival. Covid was unbidden and unwelcome. It intruded
upon the narratives of the wealthy part of the world. In technologically
advanced countries, where modern medicine is available to most, if not

all, people, we try to keep death at bay. We often ignore it, try not to think about it or think about it as an affront to the way things should be.

To be human is to be mortal, yet we are afraid of our mortality. Death interrupts, tears apart and flings us into the unknown. So of course we try to avoid it. Our fear of this final frontier, our ultimate limit, has always haunted art and literature. How do we die well? How do we live well in light of our finitude?

The final volume of J.K. Rowling's Harry Potter series lingers on those themes. The hero, Harry, has had to live with the untimely death of his parents, his godfather and his mentor, as well as threats to his own life. Meanwhile, the sorcerer responsible for all of these deaths has tried everything possible to stave off his own. Harry's journey takes him to a place of recognising that those he loved died because they chose to *live* well: they put themselves at risk for the sake of others, fought for the common good and neither treated their own life carelessly nor valued it so much that they disregarded the lives and well-being of others. This kind of coming of age is common in works of fiction; stories help us work out for ourselves what we often could not work out in the abstract.

In reality, however, we often consign these thoughts to stories and theory. One of the most popular poems to be read at funerals start with 'Death is nothing at all' (Henri Scott Holland, 1847–1918). The poem aims to comfort mourners by reassuring them that death is not the end, and that loved ones can still be cherished and not forgotten. This, of course, is true and consonant with the Christian hope of resurrection. And yet – death is *not* nothing at all. In the Christian imagination, death is so significant, so dramatic, so painful, that God gave himself in Christ to conquer it. Death is the 'last enemy' (1 Corinthians 15:26). Death is so huge that when Jesus came to the grave of his friend Lazarus, he wept. Death is not nothing. It is something that looms large and frames how we think about life, how we relate to one another, how we cherish the moments we have and use our finite time on earth.

The enormity of death explains why we are reluctant to discuss it, and why we desperately need to talk about it. The Bible is not shy about death; it talks of death in its gruesomeness and pain and also of good and timely death after a life well-lived – like the death of Abraham, 'in a good old age, old and full of years… gathered to his people' (Genesis 25:8). A life well-lived is not necessarily long, however – the life best-lived was that of Jesus himself.

Death is inherent to those who are 'flesh': 'He remembered that they were but flesh, a wind that passes and does not come again' (Psalm 78:39). Covid reminded us in the west that despite modern medicine, despite our cleverness, despite our collective wealth, we are still prey to the monsters that come in the night. Covid brought us face-to-face with our humanity. Covid also reminded us that while we are all equal in death, death does not come equally to all. The gross inequalities of our apparently wealthy societies were laid bare in statistics that showed the uneven impact of Covid in different communities: poorer, more marginalised communities suffered considerably more, partly due to underlying health fragility and partly because they were more likely to need to keep going out to work. What might the way death swept across our country tell us about how we should change the way we live?

The Bible places human life in a curious, precarious place, in between the reality of death and the promise of resurrection. We know that death has been conquered by Christ, but we do not live free from death – yet. We look ahead to the promise of resurrection, and we are called to let that promise change life before resurrection. Jesus taught his disciples to pray, 'May your kingdom come. May your will be done on earth as it is in heaven' (Matthew 6:10). The Lord's Prayer does not allow us to think of life to come, of resurrection, as pie in the sky. The kingdom of heaven is not delayed gratification but a clarion call for action today. In the curious timeline of God, resurrection has already happened in Jesus, but is not here quite yet for the people of earth. And at the same time, the resurrection promised for the end of times is already at work among us, as we are transformed and called to live the life of the kingdom here on earth.

Talk of 'kingdom' is difficult today. Kingdoms on earth have been associated with death, damage and oppression. They have tended to reflect their kings and the selfish hoarding of resources by the few at the expense of the many. Maybe this is precisely why it is important to keep thinking of 'kingdom' as we consider heaven. The king of that kingdom is a king who 'did not regard equality with God something to be grasped', but humbled himself, in the words of Paul (Philippians 2:6–7). To retain the image of a kingdom keeps human beings in relationship towards one another. On earth as in heaven, we are not just individuals with an individual relationship to the king. We are people in relation to one another, with a life together, with structures and systems to sustain that life. Therefore, to pray for the kingdom on earth is to let the vision of a perfect heavenly kingdom shape our vision for how to live on earth. To be aware of our fragility and mortality helps us think of heaven. And to think of heaven shapes how we may live well on earth.

Christian thinking on death therefore does not take us to a place of either despair or escapism, but to a place of renewed engagement with life on earth. To consider death prompts us to consider how to live well, shaped by the values of the kingdom of God.

For reflection

- What would a 'life well-lived' look like to you? How does your faith shape what that life needs to look like?

As we seek to live well, may we pray, like Cardinal Newman:

May the Lord support us all the day long,
till the shades lengthen and the evening comes,
and the busy world is hushed, and the fever of life is over,
and our work is done.
Then in his mercy may he give us a safe lodging,
and holy rest, and peace at the last.

DAY 7

Loved

'For God so loved the world that he gave his only Son, so that everyone who believes in him may not perish but may have eternal life.'
JOHN 3:16

This verse may be the best-known verse in the entire New Testament. It sums up the gospel beautifully. And yet, at the same time, human beings consistently seem to misunderstand it. Often, it sounds more like: 'For God was so cross with the world that he sent…' Other times, it sounds as if we are ignoring the 'may not perish'. Somehow, we struggle to believe that we can be sinful and finite and loved all at the same time. It is easier to either take out love or take out the reality of our frail, sinful humanity.

But the very nature of the gospel is the opposite. We are loved within our humanity. We are loved by God as people of flesh and blood, fragile, limited and embodied. We are loved as people who get it wrong, even dreadfully, awfully wrong. What we do not need to do is either try to make ourselves like God or hide the reality of who we are. We are not loved *despite* being human, nor because of what we do or how special we are. We are loved because God is God, and the nature of God is to love.

Why, then, do we find it so hard to believe? Why is it that so much of our lives and our decisions seems to be based on trying to earn love, anxiety about losing love or the sickening feeling that we are not loved at all and not worthy to be loved?

Mother Teresa captured it well:

> The greatest disease in the West today is not TB or leprosy; it is being unwanted, unloved, and uncared for. We can cure physical diseases with medicine, but the only cure for loneliness, despair, and hopelessness is love. There are many in the world who are dying for a piece of bread but there are many more dying for a little love. The poverty in the West is a different kind of poverty – it is not only a poverty of loneliness but also of spirituality. There's a hunger for love, as there is a hunger for God.[4]

The Bible tells us God loves us. The problem, of course, is that these are words. They are a promise, but promises need more than words; they need to be embodied, personalised and lived out. God's love can, sometimes, be felt directly, intensely, through spiritual experiences. But for most of us, routinely, we know God's love through the love of others around us. This is also part of being human: just as we are a whole person, body, mind, spirit all in one rather than separate parts of ourselves, we need to experience God and what we read in scripture in the whole of ourselves, in ways that are incarnated in our life story and experience. And because human beings struggle to love one another, God and themselves, they can also make it harder for one another to know what love is.

Sometimes we struggle to know God loves us because we have not been loved as children – or not loved enough as children; sometimes because of what other people have done to us; sometimes because of what we have done to others and the doubts we develop about our lovableness. There is no easy cure, other than the patient, risky business of opening ourselves up to be loved by God and by others. Our fragility, together, makes it more difficult to love one another – and creates an even deeper need to love and be loved for all of us to flourish.

When I was a probation officer, I met a young man whose story has stayed with me ever since. When I first met him, he had a real swagger. He was abrasive and defensive. He seemed quite proud of his conviction for possession of an offensive weapon. I worked hard at building a relationship – listening to his story, asking gentle questions about his home life. He was only just 18. The first time he let his guard down and told me about his mum and how sad she was he had taken up with a gang, he almost instantly bristled. He let the information slip and immediately went, 'What is this, some sort of therapy or something? I don't need it!'

More and more slipped over the weeks; you could say he kept leaking emotional information, almost uncontrollably. He had grown up in a rough neighbourhood; his mum and grandma brought him up, but he paid them little attention. His life was lived in the streets, and the streets were rough. Even before he was a teenager, he believed that the best way to be safe was to join a group of boys tougher than him. His mum and grandma tried to dissuade him, but to him, that sounded like they neither cared nor understood. By the time he was sitting across from me in an interview room, he had seen and done things he would never forget. What was most striking about him was that he did not believe anyone could possibly have his best interests at heart: not his mum, not his grandma, not his friends and certainly not his probation officer. Life was about survival in a hostile world, where everyone was an enemy. He is the most lonely person I have ever met.

I have often wondered, what would it take for someone like him to believe that God loved him? To open himself up to be loved by others? When life has hurt you so many times, it is much easier to stop believing, to stop taking the risk to open up. And yet paradoxically, the only way forward is precisely to take that risk.

Scripture tells us of a world that is profoundly anchored in God's love. God's love sustains the world; God *is* love (1 John 4:8, 16), before the world even was. God's love comes before and after us, below and above, within and without. Our entire existence is held within God's love: which means that our fragility is held gently, and that our need for transformation is safe in the hands of a God who knows us better than we know ourselves and whose call to grow in holiness and love sits within his own love for us.

Psalm 23 is probably the best-known psalm there is. The image of 'The Lord is my shepherd' is one that has comforted generations of believers. Sheep are led by the shepherd towards green pastures and still water, safe in the shepherd's leadership. And yet the reality of life on earth is not spared them as they go through the 'darkest valley'; even there, the shepherd both leads and follows, whether finding themselves in the valley is of their own making or comes as an accident of life or of the choices of others. Without ever stating that the sheep are out of the dark valley, the psalm, in its final stanzas, proclaims, 'Surely goodness and mercy shall follow me all the days of my life' (v. 6). The word for 'mercy' is also translated as 'loving kindness' – God's disposition of love towards humanity, a love that is compassionate, kind and tender. It is this love that prompts and sustains God's covenant with Israel. The translation 'shall follow me' is a little underwhelming. In Hebrew, the expression is often used in texts of battle; it is a word used for relentless pursuit of the enemy. God's loving mercy will pursue us relentlessly all the days of our lives. It isn't just that God loves us. This love is not static. It is an active kind of love, a love that seeks us out like a shepherd searches for lost sheep, a love that works constantly for the good of his people.

God's love is active and perfect, whereas ours is patchy and limited. But as the people of God, loved by God, we are called to be imitators of God. To be loved by God is to be called to share this love beyond ourselves, and, in the process, enable others to know the love of God and expand our understanding of love itself. Love between frail humans is a dangerous business – yet it is an essential business and the core business for Christians. Scripture and tradition give us tools for the business of love. The core tool may be surprising: it is forgiveness. That is, the ability to forgive others for loving us imperfectly; the ability to forgive ourselves for loving little and patchily; the ability to forgive the world for being a fragile and painful home. To love is to let go of our ideas of perfection and live with the reality of who we all are – and within it, find the treasures of God clothed in frailty. As Henri Nouwen writes:

> Forgiveness is the name of love practised among people who love poorly. The hard truth is that all people love poorly. We need to forgive and be forgiven every day, every hour increasingly. That is the great work of love among the fellowship of the weak that is the human family.[5]

For reflection

- Today, think of someone you love, someone you struggle to love and someone you need to forgive. Pray that God would help you take just one more step in your relationship with each person. What does this step look like? If it feels too big, what would a much smaller step look like? Pray for the ability to grow in love and to accept that you, and others, love imperfectly.

God whose name is love,
help us love as you do,
fiercely, tenderly,
patiently and passionately;
help us see your love in the face of those who reach out to us;
help us reflect your love to those around us.
As we learn to love,
give us the patience and grace to forgive
the world, others and, most of all maybe,
ourselves.
Amen.

2

He came into the world

In the beginning was the Word, and the Word was with God, and the Word was God. He was in the beginning with God. All things came into being through him, and without him not one thing came into being. What has come into being in him was life, and the life was the light of all people. The light shines in the darkness, and the darkness did not overcome it.

JOHN 1:1–5 (NRSV 1995)

The world that Jesus came into was not that different from our own. It was a world where human beings hurt and maim and where injustice is the norm; a world where people loved and lived and survived; a world where people prayed and longed for God. The world Jesus came into had its own geography, its own history and its own geopolitical reality. The coming of Christ is not independent or abstracted from those, but deeply embedded in the world of his day, and that world shaped Jesus as a person and gave a specific shape and texture to his ministry, and therefore to the 'revelation' that is Christ.

To follow Christ is not to come out of the world or stand above or slightly to the side of the world, but to go deeper into its reality, its beauty and brokenness. To go into the world means to be shaped in response to the world – but not defined by it. Jesus was shaped by being born in the first century, in a Jewish family, in Palestine, within a family of modest means, as a man. His teaching reflected the landscape and preoccupations of the day; it was marked by the idioms and images of his culture. His ministry responded to the social and political shape of his world: in interaction with those who are marginalised, in interaction with power, with poverty, with illness, with corruption, with stereotypes. Jesus' teaching is not disembodied. Whatever he said and did about justice, about worship, about our relationships with God and one another was embodied in a specific place and time.

DAY 8

Nazareth and Bethlehem
a world of expectation

Once when [Zechariah] was serving as priest before God during his section's turn of duty, he was chosen by lot, according to the custom of the priesthood, to enter the sanctuary of the Lord to offer incense. Now at the time of the incense-offering, the whole assembly of the people was praying outside. Then there appeared to him an angel of the Lord, standing at the right side of the altar of incense. When Zechariah saw him, he was terrified, and fear overwhelmed him. But the angel said to him, 'Do not be afraid, Zechariah, for your prayer has been heard. Your wife Elizabeth will bear you a son, and you will name him John. You will have joy and gladness, and many will rejoice at his birth, for he will be great in the sight of the Lord. He must never drink wine or strong drink; even before his birth he will be filled with the Holy Spirit. He will turn many of the people of Israel to the Lord their God. With the spirit and power of Elijah he will go before him, to turn the hearts of parents to their children and the disobedient to the wisdom of the righteous, to make ready a people prepared for the Lord.' Zechariah said to the angel, 'How can I know that this will happen? For I am an old man, and my wife is getting on in years.' The angel replied, 'I am Gabriel. I stand in the presence of God, and I have been sent to speak to you and to bring you this good news. But now,

because you did not believe my words, which will be fulfilled in their time, you will become mute, unable to speak, until the day these things occur.'
LUKE 1:8–20

Advent is a time of expectations. We say this in church a lot. But of course, it is true far beyond the church. Expectations start even before Advent. Months before Christmas, there is speculation about Christmas adverts and how good they might be. Endless adverts and decorations and promotions set up expectations that Christmas will be 'the most wonderful time of the year'. Some, like Scrooge, would rather say, 'Bah, humbug!' than enter into the game of expectations. Some may fear being disappointed. Some may try to get away from expectations: because they cannot afford the Christmas sold in adverts, because their families are not the perfect picture found in books and Christmas movies, or because this time of year is just too painful. But even negative expectations – of being disappointed and sad – are expectations of a sort.

Human beings and their communities are full of expectations, because human beings are creatures of time. We remember the past and wonder about the future; we carry with us the awareness of what once was and what may yet be. To live with expectations is to realise that the shape of the present does not have to be that of the future – for good or ill.

Stories early in the gospels are stories of expectations. Nazareth and Bethlehem, the theatre for the early parts of the gospel, were in the far reaches of the Roman Empire. They were small places, often disregarded, sometimes despised. They held small expectations and great expectations.

There were routine expectations – the expectations of parents that their children would turn out well, that they would be safe and secure. I wonder whether Joseph's expectation was that Jesus would turn out to be a great carpenter. There were the usual expectations of communities – that young women would not become pregnant outside marriage, that people would follow in the footsteps of their parents, that children and adults would live in ways that respected deeply held customs and traditions: expectations intertwined between culture and religion, between human and divine words, between lifegiving and death-condemning. The whole fabric of our lives reflects this tight weaving together of unspoken expectations that guide our choices, that shape our interactions and that sometimes come to the surface when they seem out of place or no longer relevant or when they turn into a straitjacket. It is worth, in Advent, stopping and considering: what are my expectations? What shapes them? How far do they reflect something good and holy? Are some of my expectations harmful, some neutral? How can we decide?

The gospels are full of people with expectations.

We meet Elizabeth, who had waited for a child and not let her shattered dreams turn sour. Zechariah, her husband, found that their long wait for a child had curtailed his ability to hope, so that he greets the news of pregnancy with sarcastic, but understandable, disbelief. When expectations are dashed again and again, it is often easier not to hope anymore.

Simeon and Anna, who will greet Jesus in the temple, have spent their lives waiting for the Messiah; long lives, not knowing whether the Messiah would come within their lifetime. After all, many prophets had also expected a Messiah, yet never lived to see his arrival. Simeon and Anna were waiting differently. Simeon was waiting for an end – when he sees Jesus, he knows that his expectations, and those of Israel, are fulfilled and that he can die in peace. Anna, in contrast, was waiting for a beginning: her expectation is that the Messiah represents the turn of the tide, and she goes out and tells everyone. Both are honoured in the narrative, but the contrast shows how similar expectations can hold different meanings.

Later in the gospel we meet Zealots, freedom fighters, who were also expecting God to act, their expectations shaped by their political belief of how the world could be changed: through force and might and political action. They were right to expect God to intervene, but what they expected was not entirely shaped by God. Herod and other political leaders also had expectations: they expected that some people would challenge their rule, and they were ready to respond swiftly and brutally.

As the gospels progress, we meet those who are marginalised by their life circumstances, by the actions and expectations of others, by a merciless social system: people who were poor, ill or with disabilities; women and foreigners; those considered sinners and good-for-nothing; those who played the system for their own gain. Often they barely dare to expect, or hope, like the woman reaching for the fringes of Jesus' tunic. The entire story of the gospels is a story of challenging and reshaping expectations into God-rooted and God-centred hope.

It is easy to trick ourselves into thinking that the hope of the kingdom that Jesus proclaimed should be welcome. But throughout the gospels, we find that the people Jesus meets often feel confused and sometimes hostile. The hope Jesus offers seems to undermine expectations. Even the manner of his birth is disturbing: he comes from Nazareth, a despised town; he is born to a woman who got pregnant before she was married, into a family of no notable fame. There is so little here that fits with the grand expectations of a Messiah – let alone expectations of how God himself may erupt into the world! Beyond confusion, we find outright hostility. In the gospel of John, straight after feeding the crowds and teaching them about the 'bread of life', even Jesus' disciples found his teaching difficult and 'turned back and no longer went about with him' (John 6:66).

Jesus' challenge to expectations grated and discomforted, because expectations are rooted in desire, in the deep yearnings of our hearts and lives, and human desires are notoriously fickle. It is easy to domesticate and tame the call of the gospel into something manageable, something that fits into our other human expectations and desires. But the teaching and ministry of Jesus suggests that the gospel is wild, unpredictable and demanding. It brings us up short, and questions our expectations and desires. 'What is it that you want?' is a question

Jesus asks several times, probing motives and deep desire. Do you really want to be healed? Do you really want wholeness, justice, truth? Or might they turn out to be uncomfortable, because of the change within yourselves if you are serious about pursuing them? Or even, do we have the right expectations, but the wrong way of pursuing them, as Zealots and Pharisees both found – Zealots trying to pursue hope through political conflict, and some Pharisees through human efforts.

To be human is to have mixed motives, to be deeply ambivalent about our need of God and our fear of God's purposes. But in Advent, the call is for us to let the imagination of God transform and reshape our expectations and desires, so that they can be turned into vibrant, all-encompassing hope, even if the shape of this hope is a tomorrow we can scarcely imagine.

For reflection

- What are your expectations of what life should be like for you? How were these shaped? How have they changed?

- What do you expect of yourself? Of God? Of other people?

- Are you afraid of hoping?

God of hope beyond our imagination,
may you reshape our desires
to yearn after the things of your kingdom,
in the small corners of our lives,
and in the great and powerful desires of our hearts.
May you give us vision for our communities
that stretch and challenge our ways of life,
our ideas of justice
and our understanding of who you are.
Amen.

DAY 9

Rome

a world of injustice and oppression

When Herod saw that he had been tricked by the wise men, he was infuriated, and he sent and killed all the children in and around Bethlehem who were two years old or under, according to the time that he had learned from the wise men. Then was fulfilled what had been spoken through the prophet Jeremiah:
'A voice was heard in Ramah,
wailing and loud lamentation,
Rachel weeping for her children;
she refused to be consoled, because they are no more.'
MATTHEW 2:16–18 (NRSV 1995)

In the week when I am writing these words, we heard that Vladimir Putin would be indicted for war crimes, even though the possibility of a trial is remote at best. Meanwhile, a row erupted over the treatment of refugees in the UK, with government plans to refuse asylum to anyone coming in by boat, however desperate, no matter what their rights under international law. Wars and rumours of war abound, and so does the desperate search for justice and safety of people displaced by war, poverty, injustice and terror. The idyllic picture of the garden of Eden at the beginning of scripture should have been humanity's 'normal'. Sadly, today's papers, like yesterday's, portray a different base reality to being human. Some of us may be more cushioned from the ugliness of the world than others, but the world we inhabit together is broken and has been for a long time. Injustice, oppression and war are all typical of the human condition. The question for us is: how do we inhabit this without seeing it as 'normal'?

The world Jesus came into was rife with the same problems. Weapons and systems may have changed and we might tell ourselves that we are more 'advanced', but reading scripture side-by-side with the newspapers tells us that we humans have not changed much at a fundamental level. The gospels are brutally honest about this reality. The song of Mary, known as the Magnificat, is a resounding cry for justice; Mary proclaims that the world may be broken, but God will bring justice. But the very reason her song resonates, and is needed, is precisely because the world falls short of what it could and should be.

In the gospel of Matthew, straight after the narrative of the birth of Jesus, comes the story of the magi and, linked to them, of Herod, the crazed king so intent on keeping hold of his earthly power that he orders Jewish baby boys killed. As a result, the little family with baby Jesus are on the road and become refugees in Egypt. Not economic migrants, not leaving out of choice, not asking for permission, but fleeing for their lives and hoping for people and a nation, somewhere, that would keep them safe. There is a lot of irony in the story. Go back to the book of Exodus, and you find that Egypt once was home to a tyrant king, Pharaoh, who also ordered Jewish baby boys to be killed, prompting the exodus of an entire people. Egypt now is the safe place while the promised land has turned sour under Roman occupation. There seems to be no truly safe place: all nations are equally guilty, equally prone to gestures of evil – and to gestures of costly love.

What do we do with this fact? Are violence and injustice simply to be accepted or lived with? Injustice and oppression in scripture may be a routine part of human life, but they are never portrayed as 'normal' and never normalised. They are always a subject of outrage, anger and lament – even when wider society accepts them and stops seeing the world for what it is. Failure to see reality is something the people of God are consistently taken to task over by the prophets of the Old Testament. It is easy for a society to settle and stop seeing where the foundations of its wealth lie, stop recognising patterns of inequality, stop hearing the cries of those left behind. Deuteronomy issues a stern warning to those who oppress the poor: 'They might cry to the Lord against you, and you would incur guilt' (24:15). The problem, however, is that in complex societies in a global world, the ways our economies work mask much of the ways in which workers, often in other countries, are exploited in order to provide cheap goods for the west. How often do we seek to find out how our clothes were produced and whether labourers were paid a fair price? How often do we reflect on the whole chain of people involved to bring safe food and water to our tables? Closer to home, and move obviously, we see homeless people sleeping on our streets, working people using food banks in increasing numbers and children going to school hungry.

What does the song of Mary tell us for this world? How do we avoid getting used to the way things are and normalising injustice, rather than nurturing outrage and hope for something different? One of the ways in which we can do this is to let the imagination of scripture confront us – again and again, let the oddness and jagged edges of the text discomfort us when we are too comfortable.

I teach classes on the Old Testament. And often, my students find the Old Testament difficult and challenging. They complain it is blood-thirsty, and that God is too angry and uncomfortable. Yet what if we dig a little deeper, and see how the anger of God is often associated with the evil, injustice and violence of people? And what if we asked: what would the prayers of those who are oppressed, who are treated unfairly, who go to bed hungry and see their children suffer, be? For those on the sharp end of injustice, it may be that their prayer was 'How long, O Lord?', and God's anger seemed too slow and tame to them. The same text may be read very differently by those who are comfortable and those who need justice.

Jesus came into the world and challenged business as usual. Jesus came into a world of violence and refused to retaliate. Jesus came into a world of injustice and consistently sat and ate and talked with those who were despised and left behind. Jesus came into a world of inequality and treated every person with the same love and the same challenge. It would be easy to simply reverse the reality of the day: proclaim that the oppressed are wonderful, condemn all oppressors, and reverse the dynamics of power. But this, ultimately, would not change much, because the problem is not the way things are now; it is the way human beings think and behave. The problem is the human heart. And so Jesus sits with Nicodemus and with Zacchaeus. Jesus heals an unnamed woman with a loss of blood and heals the daughter of Jairus, a powerful leader of a local synagogue. Jesus invites those he meets to be transformed. He offers a way out of an economy of struggles for power and into the much bigger, different imagination of the kingdom of God. He offers thinking from outside, thinking that challenges the entire system and offers a different way to live.

The problem is, of course, that this different way of living involves sitting down with those who are different, giving up comparisons of worth between people, and most important of all, it can only go through the path of the cross. Change and a radically different imagination, the possibility of a new normal, only comes with willingness to follow where Christ led.

For reflection

- Today, try praying the prayer of Mary as you consider your own life with God and the life of the world. How does this prayer resonate? Spend some time slowly reading the words, dwelling in them and listening to God's voice through scripture.

'My soul magnifies the Lord,
  and my spirit rejoices in God my Saviour,
for he has looked with favour on the lowly state of his servant.
  Surely from now on all generations will call me blessed,
for the Mighty One has done great things for me,
  and holy is his name;
indeed, his mercy is for those who fear him
  from generation to generation.
He has shown strength with his arm;
  he has scattered the proud in the imagination of their hearts.
He has brought down the powerful from their thrones
  and lifted up the lowly;
he has filled the hungry with good things
  and sent the rich away empty.
He has come to the aid of his child Israel,
  in remembrance of his mercy,
according to the promise he made to our ancestors,
  to Abraham and to his descendants forever.'
LUKE 1:46–55

DAY 10

Egypt
a world of displacement and alienation

Now after they had left, an angel of the Lord appeared to Joseph in a dream and said, 'Get up, take the child and his mother, and flee to Egypt, and remain there until I tell you, for Herod is about to search for the child, to destroy him.' Then Joseph got up, took the child and his mother by night, and went to Egypt.

MATTHEW 2:13–14

I wonder what Jesus and Mary thought as they fled to Egypt, with little warning and little to take with them. This wasn't really the safest way for God to come into the world. Had I been in control, I don't think I would have sent Jesus to first-century Galilee under Herod. Human beings tend to make plans to keep themselves safe, plans that are logical and thought out and that minimise risk. A risk assessment on the incarnation would have likely been a fail.

And yet – the little family fleeing for their lives is quintessentially human. Both voluntary migration and forced displacement are endemic to the history of humanity and the past of every nation or people group.

Looking back in history, we talk of 'people movements', waves of migration and invasion. But historical descriptors can easily distance us from the human reality held within them. The people movements of the past are no different from those fleeing today: refugees from Gaza, Syria, Ukraine, Afghanistan, Eritrea and many other places of conflict; refugees from Iran fleeing political tyranny; refugees from many places whose names we rarely mention; and alongside them, those we call 'economic migrants', who leave in search of a better life, but whose previous poor conditions of living often left little choice. How do we speak of today's displaced people?

Papers and social media often stoke fear of refugees, claiming that resources are too scarce to be hospitable, though the UK takes in very few refugees compared to many other nations in the world. How does the story of the holy family challenge and shape our words and responses today?

They fled to Egypt, and Egypt was a symbol of both displacement and the economy that leads to the need for displacement. As the book of Genesis describes, Jacob and his sons first came to Egypt because of a famine. The same famine led Joseph, working with Pharaoh, to hoard grain and then sell it back to the people at a price – and when they had nothing left to give to stop themselves from starving, they sold themselves and became slaves. The economy of Egypt was based on scarcity and competition, rather than generosity, hospitality and sharing. The Hebrews were forced into Egypt to avoid starvation; they were later forced out of Egypt by Pharaoh's oppression. The same economy, the same political imagination, created migration in all directions, with the same underlying dynamic of preserving and increasing the wealth of those who were already wealthy, at the expense of those who have little.

Jesus came into this world, and the economy of the Roman Empire was no different: Herod tried to keep power for himself, at the expense of the children of Bethlehem, and forced those who had little to flee. Being strangers and aliens is a frequent feature of being human. In the Old Testament, Abraham is a wanderer and the people of Israel are often on the move; they struggle to find a place in the land, experience exile and return, and meet displaced people at every turn. In the New Testament, the book of 1 Peter is written to the churches of Asia Minor, and it describes their experience as Christians in a hostile world as being 'aliens and exiles' (1 Peter 2:11). Displacement was an image that all could recognise.

If this is a commonplace, almost defining, aspect of being human, how do we respond to this reality in our shared humanity? Scripture's answer comes up again and again, in the law, in the narratives, in the prophets, in the teachings of the New Testament: hospitality to strangers and caring for the vulnerable. Hospitality and care are not the charity of the rich, but an act of basic human solidarity that recognises that all of us belong to 'all flesh' and are equally vulnerable and at risk, equally at the mercy of the accidents of life. The Torah constantly reminds the people of Israel that God 'loves the strangers, providing them food and clothing' (Deuteronomy 10:18), and that the people are to do the same, because they once were strangers themselves (e.g. Deuteronomy 10:19; Exodus 22:21). The people are reminded that they are no different from the stranger; in other words, the stranger is not 'strange' and the other is not really 'other'. The call of scripture is to see the alien or the stranger not as primarily 'other', but as primarily human.

Israel kept reading the same words, even in generations that had not known Egypt; but as a nation, as people interdependent with generations before, they had. I suspect, if any of us went back long enough in history, we would find migration and displacement in past generations and in the histories of our countries and nations. Impermanence and fragility characterise 'all flesh'. To be human is often to feel lonely, out of place, different or strange in myriad ways. The biblical answer to strangeness is solidarity and interdependence.

I wonder how it would have felt for God to have come and been the one who was 'strange', different, sometimes awkward or disturbing. God came into the world, as the stranger, the 'other' to human creatures, hoping for and relying on their hospitality. God among us was a guest, dependent on our willingness to welcome him. In his earliest years, Jesus was already being driven out, sent into hiding in Egypt.

And yet, as the guest among us, Jesus often flipped the tables and acted as host, not at tables laden with delicacies, but outside, feeding the crowds with simple bread and fish, at a last supper in a borrowed room, as a teacher on a hillside. Jesus' life started as a refugee; it would have been easy to grow up resentful or angry. It would have been easy to apportion blame or to think of life as unfair and dominated by scarcity. Instead, out of little and few possessions, Jesus shared the generosity and abundance of God himself. Away from palaces and banquets, he proclaimed that fullness of life is not fullness of possessions, that things and wealth are not something to be hoarded, but that even what is small and humble is something to be shared. Jesus also proclaimed that being different and other did not mean you could not belong; he was fully human and belonged with all those he met: the poor, the ill, the forgotten, the rich, the sinners, the religious, the Gentiles. Jesus lived among them and reached out in love, with affirmation and challenge in equal measure.

The challenge of the gospel is not simply to reach out in love, as Jesus did, as Israel was told to, but to something rather bigger and more encompassing. The challenge is to inhabit the world in a different way, to see the world not as a place of scarcity, but a place of generosity and abundance; to see those who are different as one flesh with us, their lives inextricably linked to ours; to know that we belong in the family of God and share in its joys and sorrows; and to reach out to those on the margins. In short, the challenge of the gospel is, as Paul puts it, 'to be transformed by the renewing of [our] mind' (Romans 12:2).

For reflection

- Are there people in your neighbourhood, in your church or at work that you rarely interact with or find so different that they seem difficult to talk to or understand? What do you find most difficult or threatening in another person? Could you commit to pray for one person or group that you instinctively consider 'other' this Advent?

God of the stranger and alien,
thank you for coming to dwell among us,
a stranger in the midst of humans.
Help us to recognise you in the face of all other persons
and share in the making of a different world.
In Jesus' name, Amen.

DAY 11

Wilderness
a world of uncertainty

When Pharaoh let the people go, God did not lead them by way of the land of the Philistines, although that was nearer, for God thought, 'If the people face war, they may change their minds and return to Egypt.' So God led the people by the roundabout way of the wilderness bordering the Red Sea. The Israelites went up out of the land of Egypt prepared for battle... They set out from Succoth and camped at Etham, on the edge of the wilderness. The Lord went in front of them in a pillar of cloud by day, to lead them along the way, and in a pillar of fire by night, to give them light, so that they might travel by day and by night. Neither the pillar of cloud by day nor the pillar of fire by night left its place in front of the people.

EXODUS 13:17–18, 20–22

If you visit the Holy Land today, not too far from the Jordan, you will go through an immense wilderness, dry and barren. The landscape speaks of a rugged, inhospitable natural world. If you look carefully, you will also see entire areas cordoned off. The cordons keep people away from areas littered with landmines, left over from the wars of the 20th century. The land there speaks of human forces that seek to turn the world into a wilderness. Natural and human forces combine to create barrenness and death.

The wilderness, the desert, is an image that weaves itself in and out of the story of scripture. Jacob meets God in the wilderness, twice, at a time of inner turmoil and fear. Moses meets God and learns God's name in the desert. The people of Israel wander in the desert for 40 years. Elijah the prophet flees to the wilderness for safety and to cry out to God in despair. The prophets speak of the wilderness as a key time in Israel's past – Isaiah in particular, in chapter 35, speaks of the wilderness as the theatre for God's redemptive action. And right at the beginning of the gospels, at the very beginning of his ministry, Jesus goes into the wilderness.

The wilderness is an ambivalent place: its meaning changes, and the wilderness can never be tamed or pinned down. It is a place of death and danger and the place where God is revealed. It is a place of fear and a place where the comfort of God's presence is offered. The desert is a paradox – both literally and metaphorically. Yet the desert weaves itself through human lives as a key experience and reality. The desert encapsulates both the reality of suffering and the possibility that suffering may be redeemed and transformed.

The desert in scripture is the place where transformation happens, where human beings come face-to-face with themselves and recognise their limitations and their dependence on the God who wants to walk with them, but whom they often reject. The desert, again and again, is the place where idols are smashed and truth emerges. It is the place where our false ideas of ourselves and our false ideas of God are revealed for what they are. In Exodus, the desert is the place where the Hebrews cannot provide for themselves; no human schemes or cleverness will get them through. They can either trust God or return to Egypt – and the latter is very tempting. Trusting God in the desert is a big ask, because to be in the desert is to be in a place that seems to negate everything that gives life. Trusting in the desert means ignoring everything that is logical, everything we can see and touch and feel, and choosing to trust in God's promise, in God's word, against all evidence to the contrary. Only a real God can sustain us in the desert. False gods simply cannot. Idols crumble in the desert.

Human beings have many false gods, many ideas of who God is that have far more to do with who they are, what they desire and what their culture is than with the creator of the universe, far beyond human imaginings. The French writer Voltaire once quipped: 'God made man in his image, and man returned the favour.' When we make God in our image, we limit God, limit God's power, limit our imagination of the ways of God, to the dimensions of what human beings can do and achieve and imagine; we limit God to the human beings who are vanquished by the desert. The only God who can bring life into the desert is a God far beyond ourselves.

The problem is that a God far beyond ourselves is unsettling, other, challenging. It is the God who turns over the tables in the temple, who challenges the treatment and marginalisation of those who are poor or sick, who names sin and says 'go and sin no more', who tells us to forgive our enemies and bless those who persecute us, who calls us to take up our cross and follow him, rather than promise riches, peace and an easy life. It is the God who comes in a stable and dies on a cross. To accept this God is to allow the whole of our imagination to be challenged, again and again, and learn more of who God is, of who we are, and how to inhabit a world of deserts and valleys.

The desert is the place of transformation in scripture. Isaiah 35 paints a picture full of joy and hope of the desert blooming into flowers, and the people walking on a safe road in the midst of it, safe because of the presence of God with them. What always strikes me is that it is the desert that blooms. It is the desert that is redeemed and changed. Our natural instinct as human beings is to escape the desert; we do not really want a road *in* the desert, we want a road *out of* it. But the picture of Isaiah is clear: God leads the people through the desert and transforms the desert.

A different but similar image runs through the story of Exodus. God again leads the people through the desert. Yes, there is a land of promise on the other side. But the desert matters, because it is the desert that helps reshape the people's imagination, their relationships with one another and their social structures, so that a promised future may be made possible. The desert becomes a place of blessing when the people walk with God and open themselves to God, and the promised land will turn into desert again and again as the story progresses, when the people return to the practices and imagination of Egypt despite living in the land of promise. This is an odd thing about humans: discipleship often blossoms in adversity, when our need of God is clearer, and we struggle keeping up discipleship in times of plenty, when we are tempted by self-sufficiency and the lure of making God smaller and less challenging.

None of this justifies the desert in the first place; deserts are frightening and at time death-dealing places. But they are not devoid of hope, nor of the possibility of redemption. In the Exodus narrative, the people learn the art of life amid a landscape of death. The art of life is very different from the deadly politics of Egypt. In Egypt, the strongest and richest ruled, hoarded resources and exploited others to bolster their own position. The economic logic was one of scarcity and competition, so that Pharaoh's exploitation of the Hebrew slaves is couched in terms of political necessity and the imperative of efficiency.

In the desert, Israel learns that life is not sustained by competition and that God is a God of abundance and generosity. They are fed with 'manna from heaven'. But the divine provision comes with a catch: they are not allowed to hoard, nor to store for tomorrow. Each person gets what they 'need' – whatever their need is – but nothing more. It must have been hard in the face of the barrenness of Sinai not to take enough for tomorrow, just in case. The manna undermines human logic and survival behaviour. There is an exception to the rule: on the eve of the sabbath, the people gather enough for two days. The sabbath may be an even greater challenge to the people's imagination than manna. The sabbath proclaims that even in the desert, there is more to being human than survival, more to being human than productivity, than work, than the things they have to be. In the face of death and challenge, they are invited to nurture life, to move away from the fear that gnawed at them, and spend one day every week just being human:

art, thought, philosophy, dreaming, loving, relating, musing, resting, sleeping. At least one day a week is devoted to activities that are not about production, work or money. But maybe they are still concerned with survival; not physical survival, but the nurture of mental health, of relationships, of everything that makes life worth living.

The sabbath is blessed in creation; the creation narrative culminates on the sabbath. That narrative is full of abundance: God creates far more than what is 'needed' – more plants, more flowers, more colours, textures, animals, landscapes than the minimum needed to sustain life. The invitation to share in the sabbath, even in the desert, is an invitation to share in the abundance and beauty of God's creative activity, an invitation to recognise that to be made in the image of God is to be more than people who work to survive, and to be people who can distinguish between what they need and what they desire. In the desert, the people are reshaped to relate differently to one another and to set up a different kind of economy – one that will be generous to 'the widow, the orphan and the stranger', to all those who are walking through desert times, so that life can blossom and flourish in every place.

For reflection

- What does the idea of 'sabbath' look like in your life? How might you be able to strengthen a practice of regular sabbath?

God of the sabbath,
of deserts and rich valleys,
help us to see you as you lead
in times of plenty and in times of need.
Help us to stay faithful when life goes well
and trust your guiding hand when life falls apart.
And when our vision grows dim
and we fail to see you, or ourselves, truthfully,
may you send us wise friends and counsellors
to help us rediscover
the joy of your leading.
Amen.

DAY 12

Jerusalem
a world turned towards God

Now there was a man in Jerusalem whose name was Simeon; this man was righteous and devout, looking forward to the consolation of Israel, and the Holy Spirit rested on him. It had been revealed to him by the Holy Spirit that he would not see death before he had seen the Lord's Messiah. Guided by the Spirit, Simeon came into the temple, and when the parents brought in the child Jesus to do for him what was customary under the law, Simeon took him in his arms and praised God...

There was also a prophet, Anna the daughter of Phanuel, of the tribe of Asher. She was of a great age, having lived with her husband for seven years after her marriage, then as a widow to the age of eighty-four. She never left the temple but worshipped there with fasting and prayer night and day. At that moment she came and began to praise God and to speak about the child to all who were looking for the redemption of Jerusalem.

LUKE 2:25–28, 36–38

Visiting the Western Wall in Jerusalem is one of the most moving experiences to have in the Holy Land. The wall is the only remnant of the Temple Mount complex destroyed by the Romans, a place Jesus would have gone to pray. Visiting the Western Wall connects us through stones and physical reality to long-ago history and the human story in between. Praying at the Western Wall also brings us within the ongoing stream of prayer and relationship with God that has taken place just there over the years; praying there means laying your hopes and dreams, your fears and failures, before God, alongside those of countless others. Places like these gather together the community (and communities) of faith, and invite them into fellowship, both through space and time.

There is a constant dialogue in the Old Testament between faith on the go and faith rooted in place. Faith on the go is seen in the tabernacle, the tent of meeting, journeying with the people through the desert and into the promised land. The people are wandering, often displaced, and God goes with them. And yet together with the experience of wandering, we find the longing for roots, for stability, for land. Once the people are settled, they build more permanent places of worship, including the (first) temple in Jerusalem. The physical building proclaims the centrality of God's presence at the heart of the nation. It draws people together and reminds them that they are one, and not just disparate tribes inhabiting different parts of the country. The temple was built, structured and organised to inspire awe and remind visitors and worshippers of the utter awesomeness of God, an awesomeness that could not be tamed or domesticated.

Both temple and tabernacle symbolise the presence of God among God's people and the call for the people to worship and walk with God. Yet the symbols are slightly different by being weighted towards different ends of the scale: God travelling with the people was a reminder of the immanence of God, God's constant presence, love and care for the nation. In its grandeur and awesomeness, the temple was a reminder of the transcendence of God, of God's otherness, that there was a distance to cross between humanity and divinity. God crosses the distance with humanity to come and dwell with them, but the people still have to do some work, to keep God at the centre of their community and to walk to the temple, to take up their own responsibility in nurturing this relationship.

And then, as Jesus comes, the gospel of John tells us, 'the Word became flesh and lived among us' (1:14); except that the word for 'lived' is the word for tabernacle – a tent. God came and pitched his tent among us. There is something fragile and vulnerable about God-with-us, as well as an echo of God's presence travelling in the desert with the Hebrews. Jesus later talks of his own body as a temple. Jesus is this presence of God among us.

Jesus' time in Jerusalem features the temple heavily and invites us to reflect on where and how God is placed within our lives and our communities. We often find it difficult to keep God's nearness and God's distance together, God's mystery and God's revelation, God's otherness and the fact that God reveals Godself in ways we can understand and recognise. It is easier to tip the scales towards one end of the spectrum: either overplay intimacy and nearness and forget how far beyond our ways God's ways are, how awesome, strange and challenging God is; or, on the other hand, contemplate mystery and fearsomeness to such a degree that God becomes unapproachable, distant and less involved in the small things of our daily lives. Keeping these two things together is what we are called to do, despite our human preference for easier, one-dimensional answers.

The first line of the Lord's Prayer encourages us to do just that: 'Our Father in heaven' (Matthew 6:9). 'Our Father', with an intimate word for father, *Abba*, invites us to nearness, connection, relationship and accessibility. It is a word that brings out our family resemblance to God: in the New Testament world, children (sons in particular) grow to work like their fathers, to behave and hold values like their parents'. God is 'our Father' because we are made in the image of God, and therefore there is a likeness, a family connection between us – between mortal flesh, dust and breath and God.

But then the second half of the line reverses the polarity – 'in heaven'. Heaven is different from earth; the image is about distance, difference, otherness. It is about where we might one day be, but far from our reality now. We are creatures of flesh, rooted on earth. God dwells in heaven – God is fundamentally, profoundly 'other' to us. And yet God is 'our Father'. God came to inhabit our very flesh and hold the tension between these two poles within God's very self.

Both the temple and Jesus call the community of faith to gather together. One of the most beautiful, understated moments of the gospel is the presentation of Christ at the temple (Luke 2:22–38). A week after birth, the baby is taken to the temple to be circumcised. As Mary, Joseph and Jesus go to the temple, they meet other believers, and in meeting together, their faith and perspective is enlarged. First they meet Simeon, a 'righteous and devout' man who had been waiting for God to bring salvation, to do something new. After a lifetime of prayer and learning the ways of God, Simeon does not fail to recognise God at work. The little family may be unimpressive and of modest means, but Simeon, led by the Spirit, recognises the signs. There in the temple, another person with a lifetime of learning the ways of God is also waiting – prophet Anna. She can also tell, immediately, that God is at work for redemption through this special child.

The little gathering is unremarkable to all others, yet there, in the temple courts, they are gathered around God himself. Three generations, different life experiences, different expectations, come together. Mary and Joseph have been open to the work of God, and Simeon and Anna help them see more of what God is doing. Here we have human community gathered together around God, learning and rejoicing at the work of God, helping one another recognise the signs of God at work. The temple, Jerusalem, as gathering places, symbolise this call for the people of God to come together, and their need for one another to grow into the ways of God.

All four adults have a different calling; they are called to gather, but soon they will be scattered, so that after an intense moment of recognising God in their midst, they will have to walk out into the world and recognise God as they go. For Simeon, this is an ending. He has seen God, the promise he would see the Messiah is accomplished; he can go in peace, his life well-lived, the word of God fulfilled. For Anna, this is a beginning, at the age of eighty-four. She starts telling everyone of what she has seen and what God is doing. Her calling is to share the news with all she meets and help them recognise God too. Joseph and Mary will go on their way and learn how to care for this child, for the many years that he is in their care, learning to understand God-in-their-midst and hold on to the promise, in the words of Simeon, for pain and, in the words of Anna, for redemption. Mary and Joseph are growing into learning the strange ways of God.

For reflection

- Where do you gather with the people of God? Whose voices are you most ready to listen to? How might you broaden the range of Christian voices that help you see God?

Our Father in heaven,
we rejoice in your nearness
and pray that we would know your tender, loving care.
Open our eyes to your presence
in unexpected places.
Open our ears to hear of you
in the lives and words of others.
Open our minds to know more of you
and know quite how much we cannot know or imagine.
Open our hearts to make more space for you
and for love for the world you have created.
Amen.

DAY 13

Galilee
The world of everyday

For I am about to create new heavens
    and a new earth;
the former things shall not be remembered
    or come to mind.
But be glad and rejoice forever
    in what I am creating,
for I am about to create Jerusalem as a joy
    and its people as a delight.
I will rejoice in Jerusalem
    and delight in my people;
no more shall the sound of weeping be heard in it
    or the cry of distress.
No more shall there be in it
    an infant that lives but a few days
    or an old person who does not live out a lifetime,
for one who dies at a hundred years will be considered a youth,
    and one who falls short of a hundred will be considered accursed.
They shall build houses and inhabit them;
    they shall plant vineyards and eat their fruit.
They shall not build and another inhabit;
    they shall not plant and another eat;

for like the days of a tree shall the days of my people be,
    and my chosen shall long enjoy the work of their hands.
They shall not labour in vain,
    or bear children for calamity,
for they shall be offspring blessed by the Lord –
    and their descendants as well.
ISAIAH 65:17–23

It is easy sometimes, reading certain parts of scripture, to think that life with God is all about hearing God speak clearly, meeting with God, mountaintop experiences. After all, we read of Abraham meeting with God and receiving several promises, of Jacob's dreams and him wrestling with God, of Moses and the burning bush and at Sinai, of prophets receiving divine commissions, and of the great encounters of the gospels. But of course, these are worth recounting not because they are characteristic of everyday human experience, but precisely because they are not. These encounters are special, extraordinary moments when God bursts into human lives in unexpected ways that change the direction of events.

Most of life is not lived on mountaintops; it is lived in valleys and plains and quiet, uneventful places. Most of human life consists of routine activities, living each day at a time, attending to the tasks that have to be done, many of them repetitive and occasionally dull. A lot of life consists in putting one foot in front of the other and keeping going. As the people of God, what we are called to is not to endlessly chase mountaintops, but to keep going daily and walk in the right direction.

Atheist philosopher Nietzsche, not someone Christians often defer to, nevertheless showed remarkable insight when he wrote:

The essential thing 'in heaven and earth' is that there should be long obedience in the same direction; there thereby results, and has always resulted in the long run, something which has made life worth living.[6]

Christian writer Eugene Peterson borrowed the phrase for the title of his book on discipleship, *A Long Obedience in the Same Direction*. The obedience is long and it does not waver, though 'in the same direction' still gives some room for detours and slips over time, as long as the overall trajectory, over time, remains in the right direction.

There is something fascinating about accounts of great experiences of God in scripture. In the moment, the people worship and are often moved to new statements of commitment and discipleship. The problems come when those statements need to cash out in the practice of daily decisions. Abraham receives the amazing promise of a son; but in the face of barrenness and a long wait for a child, he and Sarah try to take the promise into their own hands, and in the process abuse and misuse Hagar, Sarah's servant, and create the conditions for sibling rivalry between Ishmael and Isaac and their descendants (Genesis 15—17). Jacob, fleeing from his brother, has a dream in the desert, in which God promises to be with him always and prosper him; but he nevertheless goes forward and tries to deceive and manoeuvre to get his way (Genesis 25—32). The people freed from Egypt see God at work through the plagues and the parting of the Red Sea; yet soon they grumble about the conditions in the desert and long for Egypt (Exodus 15—18). Great, spectacular, emotional experiences are no guarantee that we are formed for the life of faith going forward.

The pattern of contrast continues in the gospels. Jesus is affirmed by God at his baptism, then is led straight into the desert to be tempted – the moment of baptism, in his case, is worked out in faithfulness in the grind of the reality around him. It is worth asking ourselves, as we journey, whether we are looking for God in the unusual experiences – or even primarily on a Sunday – or whether these experiences give direction, but the majority of the life of faith is about making decisions, living out of love, justice and compassion every day, at work, at home, at play, in sickness and in health, with friends, family, colleagues, housemates, etc. in the different landscapes of life.

Scripture often speaks of the value of small things, and of the call of all human beings for faithfulness in the small things of life. This goes against the grain of Hollywood films and celebrity culture, of hero worship in secular society and church alike. And yet, this is our call: to be faithful in the everyday. The book of Isaiah paints a picture of restoration and ideal community in these words:

> They shall build houses and inhabit them;
>> they shall plant vineyards and eat their fruit…
> like the days of a tree shall the days of my people be,
>> and my chosen shall long enjoy the work of their hands.
> ISAIAH 65:21–22

The picture is remarkably sedate and mundane. It is the picture of humanity living well, in harmony with one another, where no one seeks to make a fortune at the expense of another, where everyone contributes to prosperity and everyone enjoys the fruit of their joint labour. Human work is valued here; 'work' can be taken in a wide, expansive meaning. Work is whatever we do in contributing to the common good, to the survival and flourishing of our communities. This is another aspect of being human: to contribute through our gifts and talents, to the measure of what is ours to offer. A life of rest and idleness is not held out as something to aspire to; in contrast, the biblical picture is for a life of balance. The sabbath matters, but so does the rest of the week. A life well lived does not endlessly work and pursue productivity, wealth or status, but neither does it sit at home idle. Balancing these factors is never easy or obvious, yet it is part of the call of the everyday – whether in paid employment or not, the call is to offer the gifts that we have for the welfare of all.

The life of Jesus exemplifies this balance too; most of Jesus' life is not lived in the public eye. It is lived in the quiet of Galilee, before the start of his ministry, working, relating, resting, laughing, crying with family, friends and wider community. This part of Jesus' life is worth much, even though we often ignore it. It speaks of this long obedience in the same direction, of contribution to his community, of willingness to share in the reality of daily living. It speaks of millions of small acts within which Jesus was perfectly faithful: in negotiating family dynamics; in making work decisions; in socialising with friends; in working as a carpenter with honesty and integrity for his customers. There may be little to see and little to tell, because we do not find the minutiae of life particularly exciting; and yet these minutiae were not too small, not too unimportant, for the glory of God to take part in it.

For reflection

- What feeds and shapes your everyday life as a Christian? How often do you step back and consider how your daily life reflects the values and teaching of the gospel?

God of small things,
who cares for the birds of the air and the lilies of the fields,
help us to value every moment, every person and every task,
seen or unseen,
and within the routines of our lives
give ourselves in love
for the life of the world –
its people, its creatures and its environment –
and nurture character in every small act,
every relationship, every moment.
In Jesus' name, Amen.

3

Living the story

So all the generations from Abraham to David are fourteen generations; and from David to the deportation to Babylon, fourteen generations; and from the deportation to Babylon to the Messiah, fourteen generations.
MATTHEW 1:17

Jesus came into a world of stories. People told the story of who they were, the story of their communities, the story of their nations, the story of God. The Jesus story only makes sense in the context of all these other interwoven stories, and we can only live the story ourselves as we let Jesus' story interact with all the strands of our own stories.

To be human is to be shaped by history and live within a broader story; but often the stories we are part of are so well-known to us and so obvious that we do not stop and ask ourselves what they are. What is it that shapes us? What stories do we tell about ourselves and our world? How do the stories we tell shape how we think of God, Jesus, ourselves and one another? How do they place limits on us and shape our expectations and desires, the things we wish to avoid, and what we think possible or plausible? Which stories do we recognise as our own, and which stories do we choose to be actively part of?

DAY 14

Son of Israel
being part of a people

The angel said to her, 'Do not be afraid, Mary, for you have found favour with God. And now, you will conceive in your womb and bear a son, and you will name him Jesus. He will be great and will be called the Son of the Most High, and the Lord God will give to him the throne of his ancestor David. He will reign over the house of Jacob forever, and of his kingdom there will be no end.'

LUKE 1:30–33

I moved to England in my early 20s. I have lived in England considerably longer than I have in France, and, to be honest, I don't know how to be a grown-up in France – I don't know how the tax system works, how employee rights work, how tenancies work, apart from the fact that it is different from England. And yet I am still 'French', despite my British passport. When I am in England, people always tell me, 'You're so French!' I still haven't quite worked out what that means, other than a vague sense of 'you're different'. But when I'm in France, people tell me, 'You're so British!' – sometimes regarding the very things that Brits tell me I am so French about! (Parenting is one of these.)

Being at home in two different cultures also means that I belong fully to neither. When I am in France, I notice what is better in England (it stays green even in the summer, and people understand the concept of queuing). When I am in England, I notice what is better about France (food, public transport and snow). I am simultaneously an insider and outsider in both cultures.

Being an outsider means I notice things I otherwise wouldn't. When we grow up in a culture, it is much harder to analyse it, to have some distance from it, to really *see* it. We usually need others, from the outside or who themselves have been on the outside, physically or virtually, to help us notice what we take for granted. Fish do not notice the water they swim in – unless something goes wrong with it. Human beings are set in culture, within certain people groups who develop ways of seeing the world and describing it, which then shapes their behaviour, choices and identity. Who we are is formed in relation with one another.

Small children (infants) gradually develop a sense that they are a separate person from their mother; their ability to learn to say 'I', to see themselves as an individual, is given to them through the gaze of the parent/carer who looks at them. Even in order to say 'I', a child needs to be given the word 'I' and its meaning, in the language of its culture and the people around them. I could not speak of who I am without using language – the words 'woman', 'mother', 'sister', 'daughter', 'French' and so on are not universal. They make sense within a certain language. If you switch language, time and place, there may be equivalent words, but there may not. And the words of another language can carry subtly different connotations.

Our whole ability to see the world is shaped by the words we use to describe it. It took me a long time to learn the difference between a turtle and a tortoise – because in French there is only one word for them, '*tortue*', so to me they are one animal with slightly different variations. Conversely, French has two different words for a one-humped camel and a two-humped camel, and I never see them as the same animal. What is true of animals is even more true of big, complex concepts in politics and social relationships, in the things we believe about humanity and how we do, can and should inhabit the world.

A big question for us as human beings is: how can we learn to see the things we take for granted? How do we react to those who help us see them from the outside, as it were? And how do we discern what we should celebrate in our cultural heritage (the water we swim in), what we may need to reject, and what needs to be redeemed and transformed? No culture is monolithic – shared in exactly the same way by everyone. But there are some common features to our life today in the west: the ubiquity of consumerism, an emphasis on personal freedom and flourishing, general acceptance of market forces and capitalism, concern about equality and forms of oppression linked to identity. You may want to make your own list.

The really interesting question is: what does not appear on the list because we simply do not notice it? What would someone from a completely different time, space and culture point to as defining features of our society, and what would they make of it – for good, or bad? Our disregard for the impact of human action on the environment was largely unrecognised until half a century ago or so. Today we simply cannot ignore it anymore. And yet it is brothers and sisters from other parts of the world that have felt the negative impact of climate change first. And it is non-human inhabitants of the world who have started declining first.

By becoming human, Jesus entered such a system of thinking and being. He learnt to speak, and expressed himself in Aramaic. The language available to him shaped his words and teaching. The social world around him shaped the type of stories he told: about farmers, about fishermen, about the lives of women (looking for lost coins, making dough) and about the experience of living under Roman occupation. More widely, Jesus was a Jew, an Israelite, a descendant of David. He belonged to a distinctive culture and nation, he identified with their pains and sorrows (as when he cried over the fate of Jerusalem), he prayed and read in the synagogue, he drew on Israel's common history in his teaching, and he assumed a degree of shared understanding of the prophets and the law. Jesus was thoroughly a man of his time and place. You cannot be human without being part of this social and relational fabric of the world. And we cannot understand Jesus and his teaching unless we seek to enter this world he was part of.

And yet, at the same time, Jesus did not accept everything of the fabric of his world. He treated a centurion kindly, in a world that was at best suspicious and at worst deeply hostile in the face of Roman oppression. He treated women with consideration and affirmed their faith, in a patriarchal society. He challenged the negative treatment of those with illnesses and disabilities. He reached out to a despised Samaritan. He ate with tax collectors, shunned for their collaboration with oppressors. He both recognised the authority of Rome ('Give to Caesar the things that are Caesar's', Luke 20:25) and challenged it through his silence when accused. In other words, Jesus inhabited his culture and challenged it as someone who was both an insider and an outsider.

The challenge was deep – but we cannot ignore the *shape* of the challenge. Jesus embraced humanity, and that meant taking on living, breathing and speaking from a specific cultural, national and ethnic identity and all the ways in which this was expressed, both consistently and inconsistently around him. The embrace was challenging and costly: Jesus could not redeem the world he was part of by simply taking a stand, or speaking, or challenging. Jesus redeemed the world through the cross and resurrection. His identification with a broken world was so deep that he bore not just the cost of the brokenness, but also the cost of putting it right. He did not criticise and challenge merely from the outside, but from as deep within as one can ever get, suffering the fate of victim and oppressor alike.

In our call to take up our cross and follow Jesus, we may wonder what embracing our humanity may look like, in love for the beauty and specificity of our cultures and communities and in the shape of the challenge that may need to be discerned together with God and extended in both grace and humility. It is easy for challenge to become shrill and dismissive of the other, to cancel the other or seek their exclusion. Jesus' challenge was the radical embrace of the cross that brought together the whole of humanity in costly grace.

For reflection

- What do you think are the defining features of your own culture? Of the culture of your church? Where do these features come from? How do you feel about them? You may want to spend some time pondering how you have been shaped by wider culture, and pray for those who influence it.

God of all flesh,
who made human beings in many shapes and sizes
and gave them the freedom to develop
languages and cultures,
art and science,
beauty and brokenness.
By the power of your Spirit,
help us celebrate what is beautiful in our cultures
and recognise what is not of you,
both in those around us
and in our own views and action.
Amen.

DAY 15

Circumcised
being part of a tradition

When the time came for their purification according to the law of Moses, they brought him up to Jerusalem to present him to the Lord (as it is written in the law of the Lord, 'Every firstborn male shall be designated as holy to the Lord'), and they offered a sacrifice according to what is stated in the law of the Lord, 'a pair of turtle-doves or two young pigeons.'

LUKE 2:22–24

Jesus was not simply part of a culture; he was also part of a specific religious tradition, which he carried within his very body. He was circumcised on the eighth day, like all Jewish boys. The bodies of men marked them out, with a personal, private sign, as belonging to God and belonging to a specific human community. It was their flesh, before they could do or say anything, that held the seal of the covenant. And this sign was passed on by parents to children – soon after birth, children were schooled into a way of being in the world meant to shape them as the people of God. Of course, different families embodied this differently and to a different degree. The book of Deuteronomy instructs the community of faith on how to nurture the children in their midst. Following God is not something that is innate or instinctive. It is something to learn and practise, habits to embed through personal and community commitments, actions and rituals.

In Deuteronomy, the practices of the community of faith are embedded both in the wider world and culture – the signs and rituals they use make sense within it, as it were. And yet at the same time they are also countercultural, meant to challenge surrounding cultures and to reshape the people of God into a distinctive community. This deep reshaping cannot be done through teaching or intellectual assent alone; it needs to be embedded into life and practised by the whole person. The life that we glimpse Jesus growing up into was made up of presenting a child to the temple, circumcision, going to the synagogue, going to the temple, following festivals, reading scripture, praying alone and with others, celebrating the Passover. Many of these would have been intergenerational events gathering whole communities.

If we read Jesus' teaching now, we can see it is deeply embedded in the stories and words of the Old Testament. His challenges to those who are religious around him are often challenges to the ways in which practices meant to shape the whole of life and community – like tithing money or worshipping in the temple – could so easily be turned into flat habits, devoid of the deeper meaning they should have had. The challenge is true for any religious group; habits and practices, including praying or studying scripture, can easily become areas for powerplays or become empty of their wider meaning. It is *how* the practices and teachings shape the whole of life that matters.

It is easy to be reluctant to engage in life-shaping practices. It is easier to want to concentrate on teaching and cerebral matters; or to think about all the things we need to do outside church for a world in need; or to use practices and rituals as a way to escape from the world outside and somehow focus on our 'spirituality'. But the embodied rituals of scripture, in Old and New Testament alike, do not give us any of these options. They are practices that require the whole of our being and that demand our engagement with God, one another and the whole of creation.

If we really want to embody them, the practices can get a little uncomfortable. In the story of the last supper shared by Jesus and his disciples, the gospel of John details the command Jesus gives: 'If I, your Lord and Teacher, have washed your feet, you also ought to wash one another's feet. For I have set you an example, that you should also do as I have done to you' (John 13:14–15). Washing feet isn't something we are used to today. It feels intimate and strange – because it means personal contact, touch, vulnerability. Few churches practice it regularly. Some argue that it needs replacing with a different sign, more meaningful for today, when we no longer walk with sandals on dusty roads. But suggested replacements usually avoid touch and 'flesh' contact; they often remove the intimacy and vulnerability involved in foot washing. A friend of mine offered foot washing on Maundy Thursday and felt despondent that no one wanted to participate; this symbol of interdependent care and service was too uncomfortable. Until, that is, a little child stood up and said, 'I will get my feet washed. Jesus told us to.'

The practice of embodied teaching is something that Jesus inhabited as a first-century Jew, and something that is then passed on to Christianity as a way to shape believers. Somehow, it seems to be core to our humanity to need embodied ways to learn the ways of God. And so Jesus gives his people two more signs, two sacraments to keep performing, as a way to learn faith in the whole of our persons, as individuals and communities: baptism and Holy Communion. Both of these involve the whole of who we are, and both involve the whole community of faith. They both proclaim that faith is not private.

Baptism tells us that faith may be personal, but that it can only grow in the fertile soil of a committed community. It is the job of the whole church together to help Christians grow in faith.

Communion tells us that faith cannot be divorced from the demands of community and the realities of economics and social justice. Holy Communion is a deeply embodied practice which connects us to the fundamentals of our physicality: simple food and drink, and the fact that these are produced by interconnected people. In Communion, we all share of one bread and one cup. There are no social distinctions, no inequalities, no economic difference. All are equal as they come before God, and all receive in equal measure. How does this shape and reshape the ways in which we belong in the world? If we take Communion seriously, what does this mean for the way in which we access the necessities of life and share them with those around us, beyond the church? If Christ is at the centre of our practice of food and drink sharing in Communion, how is Christ at the centre of all other practices to do with food, drink and their distribution? Holy Communion is not simply a ritual or a memorial for the church; it is a radical call to reshape our imaginations of what the world could and should be like, just like manna in the desert. Communion reconnects us with the reality of what we need, as opposed to what we desire. It also tells us that the whole of our physical reality is part of the economy of God and relevant to how we relate to God and embody our faith.

Communion is, also, deeply intimate. Particularly before Covid, many churches shared 'one cup'. As we passed the cup round, hands touched and lips each in turn drank from the cup. Covid highlighted how vulnerable and connected Communion really is and challenged us in how we perceive one another. For a little while, the 'other' meant danger; the 'other' was a potential enemy who might contaminate me or those I love. Just as I may also be a danger to the other. This is always true to a degree, physically and emotionally. Connection with other humans is both essential to our survival and our flourishing and a constant risk. In gathering round the Lord's table, we are reminded, again and again, that the walls of enmity – between ourselves and God, and between ourselves and one another – have been broken down. Communion challenges us to embody a different kind of community, gathered around Christ. Coming back to Communion again and again reminds us of how difficult it is to do this day in, day out.

The practices of the world around us are rarely practices of vulnerability, openness, generosity and equality. Wider economic and social systems embody a very different version of the good life, the common good and human flourishing. Communion shapes and reshapes us again and again through a counter-practice, to reorientate our desires and imaginations into the ways of God.

For reflection

- What embodied practices are central to your faith? What about your local church? Why do these matter to you? Spend some time reflecting on your engagement with one practice – baptism, Communion, foot washing, or something else that is meaningful to you.

Lord Jesus,
who invited us to gather around you
and share bread and wine at your table,
may we share bread and wine beyond the confines
of our churches and those we know
and model your love and generosity
to all we encounter.
Amen.

DAY 16

Son of Joseph

An account of the genealogy of Jesus the Messiah, the son of David, the son of Abraham.

Abraham was the father of Isaac, and Isaac the father of Jacob, and Jacob the father of Judah and his brothers, and Judah the father of Perez and Zerah by Tamar, and Perez the father of Hezron, and Hezron the father of Aram, and Aram the father of Aminadab, and Aminadab the father of Nahshon, and Nahshon the father of Salmon, and Salmon the father of Boaz by Rahab, and Boaz the father of Obed by Ruth, and Obed the father of Jesse, and Jesse the father of King David.

And David was the father of Solomon by the wife of Uriah, and Solomon the father of Rehoboam, and Rehoboam the father of Abijah, and Abijah the father of Asaph, and Asaph the father of Jehoshaphat, and Jehoshaphat the father of Joram, and Joram the father of Uzziah, and Uzziah the father of Jotham, and Jotham the father of Ahaz, and Ahaz the father of Hezekiah, and Hezekiah the father of Manasseh, and Manasseh the father of Amos, and Amos the father of Josiah, and Josiah the father of Jechoniah and his brothers, at the time of the deportation to Babylon.

And after the deportation to Babylon: Jechoniah was the father of Salathiel, and Salathiel the father of Zerubbabel, and Zerubbabel the father of Abiud, and Abiud the father of Eliakim, and Eliakim the father of Azor, and Azor the father of Zadok, and Zadok the father of Achim, and Achim the father of Eliud, and Eliud the father of Eleazar, and Eleazar the father of Matthan, and Matthan the father of Jacob, and Jacob the father of Joseph the husband of Mary, who bore Jesus, who is called the Messiah.

So all the generations from Abraham to David are fourteen generations; and from David to the deportation to Babylon, fourteen generations; and from the deportation to Babylon to the Messiah, fourteen generations.

MATTHEW 1:1–17

A good story usually starts with a bang: think of the traditional James Bond chase at the beginning of each movie; a talking cat and an old wizard for Harry Potter; or the extraordinary opening sequence of *The Lion King*, with all the animals gathering at Pride Rock to welcome a newborn king. The opening grips the audience or the reader. It uses a hook to get you to keep going. It surprises, shocks, intrigues and makes you want to find out more.

You would expect the opening chapter of the New Testament to do the same. After all, this is God coming to earth! There is plenty of mystery – the king in a stable, the virgin birth, the shepherds and angels, the magi… But none of this is where Matthew starts. Matthew starts instead with something that may seem odd to our 21st-century eyes: a genealogy.

Matthew tells us: 'An account of the genealogy of Jesus the Messiah, the son of David, the son of Abraham' (v. 1). So far so good, but not necessarily a hook. Yes, there is the idea that the Messiah has arrived. After years and years of promise, this is pretty big news; though for us, 2,000 years later, it is hard to imagine what this would have felt like to hear or read. Maybe a little like a dream come true, something promised for so long that it would seem unimaginable. The rest of the sentence is what you would expect: of course the Messiah would come from the line of David and the line of Abraham. That is exactly what you would expect. The Messiah had to be part of the story of God so far, and the story said he would born to the line of David.

And yet, this muted beginning soon yields surprises. The genealogy of Jesus is not quite what one would expect. Some names might raise eyebrows – and provoke questions. Ancient genealogies rarely named women, unless a man had several children by different wives. But in a straightforward genealogy like this, you would expect an unbroken line of male names. And yet five women appear. Mary, of course, Jesus' mother, whose story is so extraordinary that it will deserve its own telling: a pregnant teenager, not married yet, with only her word and Joseph's dream that the pregnancy is a genuine, godly miracle.

The other four women who appear each have a story to tell – a story of humanity and of God's embrace of the world as it is, rather than the world as it should be. The men also tell this story, of course. But the women catch the attention, because they are all unusual in various ways, and their presence is unexpected: Tamar, Rahab, Ruth and Bathsheba. Scholars have suggested that all four have names that may be non-Israelite, and we know that Rahab was a Canaanite and Ruth a Moabite.

Tamar was Judah's daughter-in-law. She was widowed without children, and Judah refused to follow custom and expectations and let her marry his other son so she could be provided for. Tamar took matters into her own hands, pretended to be a prostitute, deceived Judah and got him to sleep with her so she could have a child. Her actions are nowhere condemned in the story (Genesis 38); she was a woman trying to survive in a harsh world and Judah had failed in his duty of care. But the story is disturbing and brings into the genealogy of Jesus complex family disputes, questionable sexual practices and the vulnerability of women.

Next, Rahab was a woman of Jericho, a Canaanite and a prostitute (Joshua 2). She gave shelter to the Hebrew spies who had come to test Jericho's defences ahead of an attack. She makes an extraordinary confession of faith and is accepted into the heart of Israel when the Hebrews conquer the city. Rahab's presence brings the Gentiles and other nations into the genealogy of Jesus. He is not a Messiah solely for the Jews; he is reaching out to the world as a whole. Rahab's story is also one of a woman trying to survive and another story of the use of sexuality as a means towards survival. But the story goes beyond this: just like Tamar, she is never condemned; instead, she is an example of faith and a symbol of grace and promise beyond Israel. Nevertheless, her pointed inclusion in the genealogy may have raised some eyebrows.

Ruth comes next, and here we again find a vulnerable woman faced with impossible choices. Ruth had married an Israelite who died far away from home as the family was trying to escape famine. She also was childless and therefore had no way to find provision or protection in her world. What's worse, she was from Moab. Moab had been a sworn enemy of Israel. Moabites were so despised that there was a strict prohibition against intermarriage. Ruth represented something that, years before the story of Jesus takes place, would have been considered wrong, dirty or shocking. She wasn't that different from the Samaritan on the road to Jericho whose story Jesus told. But Ruth, like Rahab, chose faithfulness to the people and God of Israel (Ruth 1:16), followed their customs and found herself embraced into the community of the people of God. The story of the genealogy of Jesus is a story of grace and embrace and of care for the vulnerable.

The next story, David and Bathsheba, is well known. But the genealogy is scrupulous and introduces the name of another man, Uriah, who was Bathsheba's first husband. The story is sordid – it is a story of sexual coercion and murder, as David summons Bathsheba, a king with immense power versus a woman married to a non-Israelite, therefore a woman with little power. He sleeps with her and gets her pregnant, then has her husband killed. It is a story of the worst that human beings can do to one another, a story of the gross misuse and abuse of power and the exploitation and mistreatment of the vulnerable. It is the kind of story that Jesus the Messiah has come to take to himself, carry and transform through his love and grace. It is the story of a world that Jesus has come to transform, because it so badly needs it.

The genealogy of Jesus both fulfils and disrupts expectations. It tells the story of the world as it is, without trying to skate over the difficult, painful or horrifying bits. But it is also a story that speaks of grace, embrace and redemption of even the darkest stories that can be told. It is a story that says there is nothing of our histories, personal and communal, that cannot be held and transformed by the God who loves us.

The story of the genealogy ends with Joseph, which itself is a small surprise. After all, he had no part in the physical conception. But lineage and belonging are rooted far, far beyond genetics: what the genealogy tells us is that Jesus is part of the story, that he belongs within it and that Joseph belongs within Jesus' story too. Whoever appears in that story – hero and villain, victim and oppressor, Jew and Gentile, man or woman, known or unknown, active or passive, central or peripheral, whatever our human eyes see and whatever distinctions they make, none of this matter within the economy of God. All of them are enfolded into the unfolding story of salvation.

For reflection

- Ponder your own story or, if you prefer, the story of your church. What are the parts you may want to celebrate? What would you prefer to keep hidden, that is nevertheless part of the story? Spend some time inviting God into the story and how to retell it.

God of Tamar, Rahab, Ruth and Bathsheba,
we thank you for your presence
in the most difficult part of our stories and histories;
help us hold these gently,
and let you hold them for us,
so that your grace and love
redeem what seems to be wasted, broken and devastated.
In Jesus' name and in the power of your Spirit, Amen.

DAY 17

Son of Mary

In those days Mary set out and went with haste to a Judean town in the hill country, where she entered the house of Zechariah and greeted Elizabeth. When Elizabeth heard Mary's greeting, the child leaped in her womb. And Elizabeth was filled with the Holy Spirit and exclaimed with a loud cry, 'Blessed are you among women, and blessed is the fruit of your womb. And why has this happened to me, that the mother of my Lord comes to me? For as soon as I heard the sound of your greeting, the child in my womb leaped for joy. And blessed is she who believed that there would be a fulfilment of what was spoken to her by the Lord.'
LUKE 1:39–45

'You can choose your friends; you can't choose your family.' The old adage may be true for most of us, but in some ways not quite so true of God made flesh. Still, for all of us, and for the Son of Mary, there is an indissoluble relationship, one called in the Old Testament 'flesh of my flesh', meaning related by family. Some of us rejoice in our families, with their eccentricities and foibles; others would prefer to forget or flee; still others carry with them the wounds of family for the whole of life. When it comes to family, there are no guarantees.

Families shape us and shape our lives, through the things they say and the things they do not say, the things they do and the things they fail to do, through a complex mix of nature and nurture, of what is given, chosen and fashioned over time. Families are supposed to mediate the vulnerability of a young child: babies cannot look after themselves and cannot learn to survive without those around them. Nor can they choose those who will care for them. For God to choose to come as a human child therefore means God placing himself in the same vulnerable, dependent position, needing care that would shape the new divine-human body and being in the world.

It isn't really surprising, therefore, that the gospel of Luke starts with family stories. Matthew had started by helping us see how Jesus fits into the big story of the descendants of Abraham. Luke starts by helping us see how Jesus fits into this local, particular story of one family. To become human, God had to become particular, specific, local – while still carrying the universal of the bigger story. And so Luke tells us the story of Jesus' wider family: Elizabeth, Zechariah, then Mary and Joseph. Throughout the gospels we will see little snippets of Jesus' relationship with his mother Mary and with his brothers – as they try to understand who the man they have known for so long really is. The story of the family of Jesus is a story of how God can transform family and bring family into the scope of his saving plan.

The start of the story is both sad and common – a couple, Elizabeth and Zechariah, desperate for children to love, has found themselves unable to conceive, for unknown reasons. They had got to a point where hope had fled and reason told them it was too late. The story is at pains to tell us what kind of people they are: prayerful, righteous, following the ways of God. They would make a good family, a good home. There is no reason, no explanation for their pain, and nothing that human beings can do to change it. Only something extraordinary, something different can change the course of their lives. Like other couples in the story before, including in the genealogy of Jesus (Sarah and Abraham; Isaac and Rebekah; Jacob and Rachel), the power of death and non-being seems to stand in the way of the promise of God. This is true here, and it is true again and again in the story of God's people, in individual lives and in communities, through random events and as a result of choices and actions that go against God's life-giving purposes. The history of Israel is a history of God intervening in death-giving situations – slavery, oppression, exile, unfaithfulness, injustice – and bringing life, deliverance and wholeness. It is also a story where God himself seems to act in ways that risk negating the promise, as in the bizarre command for Abraham to sacrifice Isaac in Genesis 22.

Here, we have random infertility threatening Elizabeth and Zechariah's ability to nurture the next generation in the ways of God; and just after, we have the huge risk of a young unmarried girl becoming pregnant with the Messiah – an event which could just as easily be death-dealing at a time when the sexual conduct of women was closely scrutinised and at times brutally controlled. But the story, again and again, is of God bringing life in unexpected ways.

It would be easy to imagine that this was true of the people of the gospel, in a different time, a different place, not like ours. It is easier, when faced by forces of death that seem to crush life and bring only pain, to capitulate to a logic that says nothing can be done. It is the way it is. We just have to get on with it. It sounds like this is the kind of place Zechariah got to: when an angel comes to disrupt the logic of death, he doesn't believe it. He was a righteous man; Luke has already told us this. So why doesn't he believe?

Maybe this isn't a failure of faith as much as a failure of hope. Hope is costly and risky. For Zechariah, opening himself up to hope may have meant opening himself to crushing pain and disappointment; reopening old wounds he thought had just about closed. How many times had the couple waited, each month, to see whether a child may be growing? Once the monthly cycle of hope and disappointment was finally over with the menopause, Zechariah and Elizabeth could have settled into a new life, one without the rollercoaster of emotions, a more settled life. Reopening the possibility of hope was a very, very big ask. Hoping that God may move in a family, in a relationship, in a situation we have given up hope for can be more than any of us could face. And yet we worship a God who is in the business of bringing life out of death, garlands out of ashes (Isaiah 61:3).

In both Mary and Elizabeth's pregnancies, God is doing the unexpected, bringing life where life was not yet and no longer expected. An entire extended family was invited to walk into a new path of promise and life – without knowing where the path would lead. Jesus and John the Baptist will both walk a path where death seems to negate the power of the God of life, only to see this power vindicated. Mary seems to get a glimpse of what God is doing: her song, the Magnificat, proclaims that God is ready to bring life out of death on a much grander scale, filling the hungry and lifting up the lowly (Luke 1:46–55). Mary catches hold of the reality that our personal and communal lives are intertwined, that what God does for us as individuals, as families, mirrors and shapes what God does on a broader canvas. God's promise of life is not something to hold tightly to our chests, but something to proclaim and share and connect with in the wider world.

It isn't surprising, therefore, that one of the central aspects of Christianity is to be part of a new family – the family of the people of God. Just like the families of our childhood, the fellowship of the children of God is not full of people we choose; indeed, it is full of *people*, and therefore can bring as much pain as joy, can be just as full of strife and struggle as any other family. But just like family, we do not get to choose. We are brought in relationship into one new *body*, one might say one new 'flesh', by Christ himself. To be human is to be in relationship with others whom we do not choose and learn how to allow the God of life to transform, shape and reshape us into a people of life.

For reflection

- Today, bring to mind the different people who have shaped your journey of faith, your faith 'family', whether their influence has been good, bad or mixed. You may want to pray for each, and for the way in which they have shaped you – in thanks, in sorrow or in expectation of God's touch.

God of all people,
you have brought us into your family
in fellowship with your Son,
as heirs of the Spirit of peace.
We thank you for brothers and sisters in Christ.
We lament the failures of our family
and our own failure to love.
May you renew our love for one another
and our commitment to follow you
and put you at the centre of our life together.
Amen.

4

Embodying the promise

For a child has been born for us,
    a son given to us;
authority rests upon his shoulders,
    and he is named
Wonderful Counsellor, Mighty God,
    Everlasting Father, Prince of Peace.
Great will be his authority,
    and there shall be endless peace
for the throne of David and his kingdom.
    He will establish and uphold it
with justice and with righteousness
    from this time onwards and forevermore.

ISAIAH 9:6–7

These words of promise from the prophet Isaiah are a traditional reading at Christmas, echoed in the gospel of Luke (1:32–33). Every year, we hear them and associate them with the coming of Christ. No doubt the prophet who penned these words had little inkling of quite how extraordinary a thing God was going to do. But Christian tradition, reading these words, has consistently seen within them a pointer to the birth of Christ.

The promise here is a promise of an answer to the challenges of being human in a broken world. It captures the extraordinary alliance of the power, love and justice of God and the vulnerability of how God would realise the promise – through a small child. It is a promise of God-with-us and an invitation to see a different way of being human, one marked by walking with God and embracing vulnerable power, justice and peace.

Wonderful counsellor

A wise child makes a glad father,
  but the foolish despise their mothers.
Folly is a joy to one who has no sense,
  but a person of understanding walks straight ahead.
Without counsel, plans go wrong,
  but with many advisers they succeed.
To make an apt answer is a joy to anyone,
  and a word in season, how good it is!
For the wise the path of life leads upwards,
  in order to avoid Sheol below.

PROVERBS 15:20–24

Don't judge a book by its cover. Strike while the iron is hot. Honesty is the best policy. Better safe than sorry. Curiosity killed the cat.

Popular culture is full of common-sense advice on living our lives, gathered over centuries and repeated by parents and friends until we forget where the sayings came from in the first place. Why do we do it? So much is, literally, common sense, something that barely needs saying. Many of us know the proverbs and don't need to hear them – except that someone else usually trots them out precisely when we are tempted to disregard them. *Knowing* a wise piece of advice and *taking* the advice is not quite the same thing. This, of course, is nothing new. Every culture seems to have a repository of sayings like this, which reflect in specific ways their environment and values, and often intersect with the sayings of other cultures. There seems to be an assumption that taking and giving advice is a normal human activity and that gathering wisdom that can be applied in new situations is a valuable and normal thing to do. Today old proverbs may be replaced by inspirational quotes and crowdsourcing advice on social media – but the impulse is the same.

The question, however, as always, is, what or who do we listen to? Whose advice do we heed? What voices are worth pondering? Whose advice is informed, wise and timely, rather than just the advice we wish to hear? Even 'common-sense wisdom' can get things wrong and come up with contradictory advice: 'Strike while the iron is hot' seems to advise the very opposite to 'Good things come to those who wait'. Advice cannot be dissociated from attending to specific situations and to the person actually giving the advice.

Advice is a frequent theme in scripture. Time and again, narratives explore the impact of taking advice or refusing advice, particularly for kings. Kings can listen to bad advice, which leads them and the nation into perilous situations. Ahab is said to listen to the wicked advice of his mother, which leads him into evil (2 Chronicles 22:3). Wise counsellors are praised and sought after as an important part of good governance (e.g. 1 Chronicles 26:14; 27:32). The wise counsel of Nathan leads David to repentance after he commits adultery and murder (2 Samuel 12:1–15). The son of Solomon, Rehoboam, refuses to listen to the advice of elders (1 Kings 12), prefers the more comfortable, but unwise, advice of younger men, and leads the nation into fragmentation and conflict. The book of Proverbs again and again extols the need for all, not just kings, to seek and listen to wise advice: 'Without counsel, plans go wrong, but with many advisers they succeed' (15:22).

It isn't surprising, therefore, that Isaiah's vision for a better world, a world of justice and peace, starts with the vision of a 'wonderful counsellor'. A counsellor here is not a mental health professional; it is someone with wisdom who will help direct action towards the right ends. It is something active and purposeful; it assumes that a human being on their own cannot make all the right decisions. It is part of being human to need others with more wisdom, knowledge and discernment to help guide us. It is also human to need others to help us deliberate over the right course of action, not necessarily because of a lack of wisdom, but because together there will be more perspectives, we will see more of reality, and we will consider a problem from a greater variety of angles.

There is something liberating about this vision of humanity: we do not have to do it all alone; it is normal, wise and desirable to seek the help and counsel of others. Equally, there is something deeply countercultural about the idea that my thoughts and desires cannot, on their own, necessarily lead me into the right places, that my opinions are not necessarily right or valid, that the wisdom of a community and shared processes of discernment are needed for us to live life well and discern how to live godly lives. I wonder how good our communities are at recognising wisdom in their midst. And how good our communities are at encouraging healthy processes of discernment, in interpersonal relationships, in small groups and as whole communities? Where do you seek advice, and how do you weigh up advice and recognise wisdom?

Isaiah does not just state that there is a need for counsel. He prophesies the coming of a wonderful counsellor, or a 'counsellor of wonders'. Human wisdom on its own is always limited. Wisdom needs an ongoing dialogue with the God who knows more, and better, than we can ever do. 'Wonderful' here refers to something that causes amazement, something that surprises, something that points to the supernatural, something far beyond the realm of normal experience. It is the word used of miracles in the Old Testament. In other words, God's ways are far beyond our ways (Isaiah 55:8–9). God's counsel is likely to surprise, and at times maybe even contradict, our common-sense, earth-bound wisdom.

The child whose coming is promised will be a 'wonderful counsellor' – but his counsel will go via the way of the cross. It will go against the expectations and the desires of many. The apostle Paul will later speak of the way in which the cross is seen as foolishness and a stumbling block by those who consider themselves wise. The gentle, self-giving, wisdom of grace goes against the logic of competition and violence of a broken world. It calls the people of God to develop a different way of living and a different wisdom for living. The provocative, radical, wisdom of God is so hard for human beings to follow that we need both the wonders of God – the work of his Spirit – and one another to keep glimpsing how to be God's people in a world that would rather follow its own way and forget the cross. But the promise of God is that the Spirit will be a counsellor who leads us on the way: lead and not coerce, invite and not override, but always be present, so that to be human is to walk by God's counsel and alongside God's counsellor.

For reflection

- Where do you seek advice, and how do you weigh up advice and recognise wisdom? Does your community or church have ways in which it seeks and recognises wisdom together? How helpful do you find this?

Wonderful Counsellor,
lead us into all truth and wisdom.
Lighten our path with your word and your Spirit,
and open our hearts to the challenge of living life according to
    your ways.
Help us listen to one another and cherish the wisdom of the people
    of God.
May we welcome good counsel,
discern wisdom
and live with open hearts
even when wisdom and counsel are uncomfortable,
for our ways are not your ways,
yet we wish to talk in the ways of truth.
In Jesus' name, Amen.

DAY 19

Mighty God

Let each of you look not to your own interests but to the interests of others. Let the same mind be in you that was in Christ Jesus,

who, though he existed in the form of God,
did not regard equality with God
as something to be grasped,
but emptied himself,
taking the form of a slave,
being born in human likeness.
And being found in appearance as a human,
he humbled himself
and became obedient to the point of death –
even death on a cross.

Therefore God exalted him even more highly
and gave him the name
that is above every name,
so that at the name given to Jesus
every knee should bend,
in heaven and on earth and under the earth,
and every tongue should confess
that Jesus Christ is Lord,
to the glory of God the Father.

PHILIPPIANS 2:4–11

Power is one of those things we fear in others and often secretly (or not so secretly) want for ourselves. Power permeates everything in human life. We all use power every day in myriad ways: we exercise the power of our minds in interactions; we use the power of our humanity over nature as we collectively harness natural resources for human use; and we exercise power in relationships as we negotiate our lives together in families, in communities, at work. Power is neither good, nor bad. It is a fact of life. The ways in which power can be misused, however, often lead to a reduction of 'power' to 'force' – or to the misuse of power in ways that erase or violate the agency of others.

It is complex to assess, however. Simply overriding agency is not necessarily negative: an order of evacuation in the face of natural disasters overrides individual agency to a degree, but it is necessary to protect lives. Human beings live in communities, and community presupposes handing over some of our own power to make decisions and choices or to exercise justice, for instance, to the state or local authorities. Human community is made possible through the appropriate use and laying down of power in complex and subtle ways.

Human beings often struggle to assess their own power accurately – at times overestimating the degree to which they can make a difference, and at other times underestimating the ways in which they can influence and shape situations, even if they do not have the ability to override other forms of power.

1 Timothy 6:10 says that the love of money is 'a root of all kinds of evil'. It may be truer to say that the love of power is the root of all kinds of evil – money being a form of power. It is love of power that leads to its accumulation and use at the expense of others.

So what do you do if your power is limitless? History seems to support the old saying that power corrupts and absolute power corrupts absolutely. The more power one has, the harder it is to lay it down, the harder it is for those around to speak truth, and the easier it is for the one with power to start believing they deserve or own it. Jesus came as a baby. At first sight, it seems to be a complete divesting of power. And yet, Jesus was still God and therefore utterly, absolutely powerful. In order to lay down power, you need to have power. Laying down power is an act of power in and of itself. And in the ministry of Jesus, we see power at work in signs and wonders, in healing and deliverance, in the gift of a teacher whom others listen to, in the gift of a charismatic personality. Jesus was a person of immense power.

The prophecy of Isaiah speaks of a 'mighty God'. The word 'mighty', in Hebrew, is most often applied in military contexts. It is the power to bring about what you want to see happen. It can be brute force. 'Mighty God' suggests immense power. There is no apology and no shying away from the reality of power in God and in the long-awaited Messiah. Salvation is an act of power on God's part.

Yet the manner of God's act of power invites human beings to see power differently; it opens the possibility of the redemption of power away from a constantly frightening risk of misuse into a positive force for the transformation and renewal of all creation. The Mighty God does not come with lightning and thunder to override human choices and agency. The Mighty God does not come in ways that will maim and abuse bodies and minds. The Mighty God does not come in ways that cancel human voices or write off those who struggle. Once again, we turn to other parts of Isaiah:

> A bruised reed he will not break,
>   and a dimly burning wick he will not quench;
>   he will faithfully bring forth justice.
> ISAIAH 42:3

Isaiah brings together the immense power involved in the faithful bringing of justice and the gentleness with which God tends to human creatures.

The life, death and resurrection of Jesus tells the story of a clash between different ways of holding power. The cross is a monument to the human misuse of power. On the cross, justice is undone, human power is abused and misdirected away from the good of the community. The life of Christ, on the other hand, is a testimony to the fact that it is possible to use power differently in human relationships: to invite rather than coerce, to heal rather than maim, to teach and build up and foster growth and agency in others. Jesus Christ inhabits power faithfully.

Jesus' example sounds good, until it comes up against the sharp reality of the misuse of power around us. When faced with gross injustice, with conflict and war, with mass displacement, with horrendous abuse, with slavery, the human response is often to pray, 'How long, O God?', 'Why?' or 'Smite our enemies!' How should Mighty God respond to the horrors of human evil? It is easy to expect judgement on the actions of others – and grace for our own failings. But what about the reality of climate injustice, which creates untold hardship and fosters conflict and mass displacement in nations often far away from those that are most responsible for global warming? What if those nations pray, 'How long?' or 'Smite our enemies'?

When I teach on the Old Testament, students often complain that the God described there can sound vengeful and harsh. But in the Old Testament, there is a constant stress on God withholding judgement, on 'staying his hand' for the people's sake – until judgement becomes unavoidable because of the evil that takes place. Those who are suffering long for judgement, for a show of divine power, for justice. Judgement is not the sole purview of the Old Testament. There is plenty of talk of judgement in the teaching of Jesus, such as in the parables of weeds among the wheat (Matthew 13:24–30), of Lazarus and the rich man (Luke 16:19–31) and the sheep and the goats (Matthew 25:31–46). There is no justice without judgement, because to do justice involves making a judgement on what is right and wrong. To do justice is an inescapable act of power – and one of the characteristic actions of Mighty God. Calling on Mighty God is simultaneously fearful and hopeful.

Jesus embodies the Mighty God of justice and the God of the cross, and, by uniting judgement and grace, brings together immense power and a redefinition of how this power is used. In the life of Jesus, we see quite how seriously he takes judgement. There is no easy 'get-out clause' for those who are challenged: Zacchaeus changes his ways; the woman caught in adultery is told to go and sin no more; the disciples are challenged repeatedly about their lack of faith and their lack of understanding of the ways of God. Jesus invites them into life – but it is a different life, one that involves acting, thinking and loving in very different ways. And yet Jesus does not impose or coerce; he brings justice, ultimately, not by overpowering others, but through taking the consequences of sin on himself and invites change at a much more profound level than could ever be achieved through might alone.

And this may be the most challenging aspect of Jesus' life: he challenges the idea that true, lasting justice and peace could be possible merely through might and overpowering the other. The only possible hope goes, instead, through the way of the cross.

For reflection

- What do you think of when you hear the word 'power'? What power do you think you have, and when do you see yourself as lacking power? What does using power well mean for you?

Mighty God,
whose power is displayed for all to see
in creation, and in the cross and resurrection of Jesus,
teach us to use power wisely,
to recognise our own agency and influence,
to treat others gently,
yet to pursue justice and truth fiercely.
Teach us to hold together love and justice,
truth and grace,
cross and resurrection. Amen.

DAY 20

Everlasting Father

Philip said to him, 'Lord, show us the Father, and we will be satisfied.' Jesus said to him, 'Have I been with you all this time, Philip, and you still do not know me? Whoever has seen me has seen the Father. How can you say, "Show us the Father"? Do you not believe that I am in the Father and the Father is in me? The words that I say to you I do not speak on my own, but the Father who dwells in me does his works. Believe me that I am in the Father and the Father is in me, but if you do not, then believe because of the works themselves. Very truly, I tell you, the one who believes in me will also do the works that I do and, in fact, will do greater works than these, because I am going to the Father. I will do whatever you ask in my name, so that the Father may be glorified in the Son. If in my name you ask me for anything, I will do it.

JOHN 14:8–14

If I asked what comes to mind when I say the word 'father', every reader would have a different mental image, made up of personal experience, cultural images, wishes and fears. The language of 'father' to speak of God is common in the church, but less so in scripture. Using a human image to speak of the divine is always a perilous thing, because an image attempts to narrow the gap between ourselves and God, to make God more understandable, more like our human selves so we can catch a glimpse of God's ways with humanity. There is nothing wrong with this, of course – human language and images are the only language and images we have. God entering humanity in Christ gives us even more ground for speaking of God in human images and language.

And yet there is a danger if we forget that whatever language we use is only analogical, telling us that God is a *little bit like* something we know as human beings. But because God is God, he will always be more, and beyond, whatever we can say and capture into words. The language of 'father' is a case in point. Our pictures of fathers are shaped by our experience of them, good and bad, and by what our cultures say fathers are or should be. It is easy to project these ideas on to God and imagine that God is like the fathers we know, want or fear. And if we do, there is only a short step towards expecting that others should see or experience God in this exact way too.

The language of 'father' invites experience into our concept of God, because everyone has a father – whether they have been present or absent, positive, negative or neutral, they will have shaped some of who we are. Other images, like 'shepherd', 'counsellor', 'refuge', 'lion of Judah' and 'lamb', are not quite as laden with emotional baggage. To speak of God as Father is to use an image that cuts straight through to intimate experience, identity, love and relationships. To use the image is a vulnerable thing to do, because we bring with it much of who we are and how we have been shaped to be. It is also an image that invites us into a relationship with God that is closer than friends or disciples. It invites us to recognise ourselves as children of God – therefore shaped by God, brought into being by God, and brought into relationship with one another through the God we share. It is no small matter.

Some will embrace the language joyfully, either because they have enough positive experience of their own father or of being a parent themselves or because God may have replaced a difficult or absent parental figure. Others, like me, will find the language difficult and avoid using it, because of difficult experiences or discomfort with the way in which societies over time have given immense power and status to male heads of households in ways that have been abusive and destructive.

What do we do with this promise of an 'Everlasting Father', then? Maybe this is a promise like many others, ambiguous when we stop and think about it carefully, a promise that challenges our expectations. The most famous use of 'father' in scripture and tradition comes with the words of the Lord's Prayer: 'Our Father in heaven, hallowed be your name.' 'Our Father' is the language of intimacy, of a child towards a parent they know well. It is language that collapses the distance between God and humanity. It is also language that brings together a vertical relationship with God (Father) and a horizontal relationship with all God's children ('our'). Yet the next part of the prayer, 'in heaven', catapults us into a completely different plane – immediately, distance is re-established! And 'hallowed be your name' further cements the sense of difference and distance between God and humanity. Somehow the Lord's Prayer invites us to see God as both this close intimate, loving presence *and* this transcendent other, far beyond what we can imagine or comprehend. God is both a little like the fathers we know and immensely different from them.

The same thing occurs in the words of Isaiah 9:6, 'Everlasting Father'. Human fathers are limited; they are only alive for a little while; they grow old and die, though the memory of their presence or absence often leaves deep marks in our lives. Yet God is an 'everlasting father'; there is no shadow of absence, of abandonment or grief here. Time is collapsed, and God's intimate presence with us, his guidance, his watching over his children, extends into eternity. The father that God is, is in many ways more unlike than like the human fathers we know – but the word is an invitation to come and get to know him more and, in the process, discover more of who we are.

The story of Jesus invites us to discover not just more of who God is, in ways that human beings can understand, but also more of who we are and can be. The promise of a Saviour is the promise of a God who embraces humanity and keeps humanity and divinity held closely together. It is tempting maybe to want to look for only the best of humanity, only those things that we cherish or that we have experienced as good. But Jesus embraces the whole of humanity and redeems what has been broken and disfigured, so that we do not need to deny or transcend those parts of human experience, but can embrace them too, in the knowledge that God holds us safe in his hand.

For reflection

- What images of God do you find easiest to relate to? Which images do you tend not to use? Why do you think that is? Today, could you try to pray while holding in your mind a different image of God – good shepherd, friend, Lord, counsellor, lion of Judah, etc. – and be attentive to how this shapes your praying?

Everlasting Father,
in whom there is no shadow of change
    or abandonment,
we thank you for your close presence,
for your care and gentleness,
and for the direction you give to our lives.
Expand our understanding of who you are,
heal the pain of experiences that overshadow
    our relationship with you,
and bring us to new places
where we can come to know you anew.
In Jesus' name, Amen.

DAY 21

Prince of peace

And you will hear of wars and rumours of wars; see that you are not alarmed, for this must take place, but the end is not yet. For nation will rise against nation and kingdom against kingdom, and there will be famines and earthquakes in various places: all this is but the beginning of the birth pangs.
MATTHEW 24:6–8

Watching the news is a bracing exercise. It can feel like a relentless stream of negativity, but it is a good way to remind ourselves of the Bible's diagnosis on the human condition: 'All have sinned and fall short of the glory of God' (Romans 3:23). The world is broken, and not just human beings: news bulletins report war, conflict, inequality, injustice, and the abuse and ravaging of creation. It isn't simply that individuals make wrong choices, but the whole of creation, all human systems and the ways they interact with one another and the wider world are touched by pervasive malfunction. The apostle Paul talks about all creation 'groaning' in 'eager longing' for the redemption of all things (Romans 8:19–23). The redemption of all things involves deliverance, or salvation, but goes far beyond a mere escape from what is bad or broken. The picture Paul paints is of the renewal of all creation, a new order where God reconciles all things to himself (Colossians 1:20). In the Old Testament, the concept is captured in one word: *shalom*, or 'peace'.

'Peace' is a slightly anaemic translation. The Hebrew word contains a host of connotations and ideas behind it, and it is anchored in the whole story of God's faithfulness to, and covenant with, the people of earth. It can mean peace, safety, soundness, health, wholeness, wholesomeness, well-being, welfare, prosperity, security… In other words, 'peace' is everything that makes for the flourishing of creation. One of my friends, bishop Anthony Poggo, who comes from the war-weary country of South Sudan, once told me that for him, peace is 'sitting outside my house, under a mango tree, while my children are safely at school, learning'. Peace makes life and flourishing possible. Yet peace comes at a cost, too.

The root word for peace also gives another, related Hebrew word – recompense, or repaying, requital. Peace can only happen when wrongs have been put right: there is no peace without justice, and no justice without an understanding of the right and healthy ways of living.

Isaiah puts it like this:

> The effect of righteousness will be peace,
>   and the result of righteousness, quietness and trust for ever.
> My people will abide in a peaceful habitation,
>   in secure dwellings, and in quiet resting places.
> ISAIAH 32:17–18

When we pray for peace, we pray for more than an end to conflict. We pray for a different order of things, for a different way of living. And this is where human beings usually struggle. Negotiations and exhaustion from fighting can bring an end to hostilities, but to bring peace, a new world needs to be imagined, which involves laying down the ways of thinking and behaving that led to conflict in the first place. The story of the Hebrews in the desert illustrates the point. The challenge for the people was not just to escape Egypt, but to be able to create a new life that did not simply replicate the economy and values of Egypt. They keep struggling as the story goes on – once they find land and try to settle it, ongoing conflict with surrounding nations constantly threatens their survival. But at times of 'peace', their survival as a distinctive community of God's people is still under threat, because they are always tempted to follow the practices and beliefs of their neighbours, and to do only 'what is right in their own eyes' (Judges 21:25). In peace time, Israel discovers that the work of peace is costly and demanding. It requires the conversion of their entire imagination, of the ways in which they think about the world, God and themselves. Without this conversion, injustice and conflict will keep being the dominant feature of the community as different interest groups vie for power rather than pursuing the flourishing of all.

Peace therefore is about human relationships; the promise of peace is made to human communities. Whether scripture speaks of today or of a renewed future in heaven, human beings are relational and communal. The image of the kingdom of God, where the Son of God is the 'Prince of Peace', is an image of an organised relational community. 'Kingdom' implies systems, organisation, relationships beyond self and close friends. It implies a political and social community. God is love, the New Testament tells us (1 John 4:8). If the essence of God is love, if love defines the entire being of who God is, then God is essentially relational. One cannot love alone. And if human beings are made in the image of God, then this relationality is also at the core of humanity.

This is challenging! Often it can feel as if life would be easier with just a small group of like-minded people; it can be tempting to want to escape or retreat from society and the complexity of human beings trying to live well together. But, as one of my friends often says, if you retreat to the desert in order to escape the world, you will meet Jesus going the other way! This is not because times of retreat are wrong, but because setting time aside to search for God and nurture spirituality should lead us to love the world more deeply and engage with it more fully. Seeking God is about openness to be transformed so that our imagination, our faith, our understanding of the world and our relationships are shaped according to God's call for justice and peace.

Because Jesus is the 'Prince of Peace', he calls his followers to fashion their lives in the same way: 'Blessed are the peacemakers, for they will be called children of God' (Matthew 5:9). Images of peace in the Old

Testament are often earthy and practical – like my friend's mango tree. They are pictures of ordinary people living and loving well. Often the pictures are domestic and simple:

> They shall build houses and inhabit them;
>> they shall plant vineyards and eat their fruit.
> They shall not build and another inhabit;
>> they shall not plant and another eat;
> for like the days of a tree shall the days of my people be,
>> and my chosen shall long enjoy the work of their hands.
> They shall not labour in vain,
>> or bear children for calamity;
> for they shall be offspring blessed by the Lord –
>> and their descendants as well.
> ISAIAH 65:21–23

The image is striking, because it is not an image of the powerful doing great things. It is an image of ordinary people living ordinary, healthy, fulfilling lives. It suggests that peace is found not in pursuing excitement or greatness, but in being fully human, with families, friends, meaningful work and in harmony with creation. And one of the keys to the many passages of new creation in Isaiah is that there is no longer mention of human kings or leaders. Instead, nations and communities gather around God himself, and the presence and rule of God are what enable peace, well-being and fullness of life to blossom.

For reflection

- What does 'peace' look like, in your opinion? How does Isaiah's vision of peace match with yours? How might the words of Isaiah help you pray for peace for your own community, nation and the wider world?

Prince of Peace,
we pray for people of peace,
made in your image
and following in your footsteps
to model and lead new ways of living,
in war-torn countries,
in poverty-stricken places,
in places of inequality
and of hidden oppression.
May you transform our desires
and our vision
so that we may pursue
all that makes for godly peace.
Amen.

Authority

A shoot shall come out from the stump of Jesse,
  and a branch shall grow out of his roots.
The spirit of the Lord shall rest on him,
  the spirit of wisdom and understanding,
  the spirit of counsel and might,
  the spirit of knowledge and the fear of the Lord.
His delight shall be in the fear of the Lord.

He shall not judge by what his eyes see
  or decide by what his ears hear,
but with righteousness he shall judge the poor
  and decide with equity for the oppressed of the earth;
he shall strike the earth with the rod of his mouth,
  and with the breath of his lips he shall kill the wicked.
Righteousness shall be the belt around his waist
  and faithfulness the belt around his loins.

ISAIAH 11:1–5

Isaiah, like other prophets, is deeply concerned with the structures of society. How people relate to one another, and how this is shaped and facilitated by those in power, is a key theme in prophetic books. Usually it leads to negative reflections: those with power rarely use it as well as they should. Yet power, authority and leadership are intrinsic to human societies: complex organisations need coordination and leadership to thrive, by enabling all to work together towards the common good. Isaiah considers the cluster of concepts that enable flourishing communities – power, love, peace, justice, righteousness and 'authority': 'Authority rests upon his shoulders… Great will be his authority, and there shall be endless peace' (9:6–7).

The word 'authority' doesn't have very good press today. It quickly conjures up negative memories of school or, on a bigger scale, pictures of totalitarian rulers oppressing populations under their care. The word Isaiah uses can mean authority, leadership or government – it is the action of enabling the life of a community or nation through the proper discharge of responsibilities. All the words Isaiah uses in this passage need to be held together in order to understand the promise. 'Authority' or 'government' divorced from justice and righteousness, divorced from responsibility and duty, is necessarily abusive. The picture of leadership that Isaiah gives is a picture of the redemption of authority. It is a picture similar to that of the good shepherd.

Authority has a bad press because we know all too well how often it is abused. But its negative connotation may also be rooted in something else. The exercise of authority mediates individual and communal needs. As a result, it inevitably asks us to foreground our responsibilities rather than our rights and to restrain the exercise of our passions and desires. When I was at school, in France, we had to do citizenship education, and our teacher repeated again and again that we only have rights because we grant one another those rights and live up to the responsibility of respecting rights. He also kept telling us that an individual's freedom stops where another's begins. Yet contemporary western culture emphasises personal rights and freedom to a much greater degree than most other civilisations. Individuals often speak of their rights far more than they speak of their responsibilities towards others. The world of scripture goes the other way. It speaks far more of our duties and responsibilities to our neighbours, because it is when we take these seriously that we create the space for all to thrive and for individuals to be nurtured.

The book of Judges is fascinating in this regard. In many ways, it is a book about leadership and the flaws of leadership. Leader after leader finds that power is a heavy burden and that their own personal vulnerabilities lead them astray. It is also a book about the complex web of interwoven responsibilities between leader and people, and the ways in which support for leaders means that they cannot be blamed in isolation for their failures, in that their abuses of power reflect a complex ecosystem of beliefs, culture, actions and attitudes.

At the beginning of the book, the people are all looking towards God and reaffirm the covenant. Their responsibilities towards one another are foregrounded. As the book progresses, the people increasingly 'do what is right in their own eyes' and 'what is evil in the eyes of the Lord'. Instead of holding a sense of the common good between them, personal choice and desires increasingly shape the conduct of leaders and people alike. Individual choice becomes more important than social responsibility. Paradoxically, in the logic of the narrative, the more individualistic the nation becomes, the more vulnerable its individual people are. By the end of the book, individual lives are worth little, and the most vulnerable – women and children – are treated with utter disregard, while overall leadership disintegrates. This is not as paradoxical as it may sound: the only way to protect individuals is for the group to agree on standards of behaviour and values that protect all, especially those who are more vulnerable, which inevitably restricts personal action.

Achieving the right balance between rights and responsibilities, between individual and group, is of course extremely difficult and comes out of negotiation and ongoing discernment. There is always a risk that group expectations may become tyrannical and crushing, particularly towards minorities. But it is worth reflecting in the context of our present society, how do we balance these things? What are our responsibilities towards others, in the nation, and within the community of faith? How do we discern what restrictions on personal choice are appropriate?

Isaiah's picture is one that transforms the understanding and symbolism of authority: it starts with a little child. The metaphor only begins in Isaiah; Christian readings bring Isaiah's prophecy together with the story of the life, death and resurrection of Jesus Christ. In this story, the entire concept of authority/power is reshaped and turned on its head. Jesus is said to have authority – over demons and forces of evil. He has authority over the powers of nature, too, as he calms the storm, walks on water and feeds the crowds. But this is an authority exercised solely for the benefit of others. Jesus' authority as a teacher grows as many come and listen and ask for advice. Yet he never violates the agency of his disciples. They are free to listen and follow and are free to go, as many do when they find his teaching too hard. Jesus' teaching is authoritative because those around him can see that his teaching and his deeds match, that his teaching and life bring out the best in those who follow.

Jesus' authority rests on gaining the respect and trust of those around him. It is deeply personal and relational. People trust people. Maybe this is part of the challenge for human beings today: our systems tend to be large, complex and far removed from the people they affect. This makes it harder to trust and harder to hold accountable. But the promise in Isaiah is that it is possible for government and authority to be fundamentally good, right and just – when it is centred, first and foremost, on the person of Jesus Christ and his life of self-giving for the sake of others.

For reflection

- What duties and responsibilities do you think you have as a Christian towards the church locally and globally? How do you feel about these? Where have these ideas of duty and responsibility come from?

Good Shepherd,
on whose shoulders rests all authority,
may we accept your gentle rule
and recognise the limits of our own judgement.
Help us serve our communities and nations,
and foster the flourishing of all
in the way we live, individually and communally.
Amen.

DAY 23

Justice and righteousness

'With what shall I come before the Lord
    and bow myself before God on high?
Shall I come before him with burnt offerings,
    with calves a year old?
Will the Lord be pleased with thousands of rams,
    with ten thousands of rivers of oil?
Shall I give my firstborn for my transgression,
    the fruit of my body for the sin of my soul?'
He has told you, O mortal, what is good,
    and what does the Lord require of you
but to do justice and to love kindness
    and to walk humbly with your God?

MICAH 6:6–8

I once heard that the best way to cut the last piece of cake in two absolutely equal pieces is to ask your older child to do the cutting and the younger child to pick which half they want. Children have a very strong sense of fairness, or maybe more accurately, of unfairness. They are quick to complain, 'But it's not fair!' at perceived injustice or (to their mind) unreasonable demands.

Where do we get this sense that justice, fairness and equality are so essential? Is it mostly self-preservation or is there something deeper, rooted in the image of God within us? God is love, John tells us. That God is love is evident in the ministry of Jesus: the whole life and ministry of

Christ is predicated on self-giving for the sake of the other, on forging a path to lead towards the flourishing of all. But this love-in-action has an edge; Jesus does not offer a first-century supernatural equivalent to the NHS, with free healing and counselling. His presence is challenging and focused beyond the individuals he interacts with. Jesus attends to persons-in-relationships and to persons-within-structures. And this attention means that the love-in-action embodied in Christ speaks of justice and righteousness as non-negotiable elements of the deliverance and redemption of human communities. Individuals are not only caught up in their own sin and brokenness, but also inextricably enmeshed in systems, cultures and behaviours that can damage and destroy or enable to flourish – and sometimes both at the same time and in different ways.

Jesus therefore challenged systems of injustice and challenged individuals to see, think and behave differently. It all starts with noticing – usually through seeing or hearing something that is largely ignored: the plight of a beggar on the side of the road (John 9), the plight of a man without friends to help him get into the pool of Bethesda (John 5:1–16), the plight of a woman with a chronic loss of blood who dares not ask for anything (Luke 8:43–48). Jesus notices those who are not noticed by others and brings them to the attention of those around. We often read these episodes as focused on the individuals being healed, and yet it is rarely the individuals that most need healing; it is the crowds watching, the disciples, those who had learnt to ignore, despise and marginalise sections of the population. There is no privatised faith in the ministry of Christ. To follow Christ is to be engaged in the transformation of all things, to allow our social relationships to be reset, reconfigured and redirected towards the flourishing of all and the care of those who matter least in the eyes of the rich and powerful.

This is not surprising. The Old Testament – the Bible Jesus read and the revelation of God over millennia – has a consistent focus on 'justice and righteousness'. The words usually appear together. The pair, taken together, direct us towards two aspects of what we call justice in English: reactive justice, the response to what goes wrong, and proactive justice, or social justice, establishing and deeply embed-ding the types of behaviours, attitudes, values and systems that will enable the common good. Justice is therefore about systems and people, about actions and attitudes, about the inner disposition of the heart or our desires, and about the ways in which our life together is organised and regulated.

When Isaiah promises a Messiah who will bring about justice and righteousness, we instantly think it is something to celebrate. And it is. But it may also be something deeply challenging and difficult. To bring about justice means to bring about judgement, too: judgement on what is wrong, on what brings death and dysfunction, on sin in our societies, our economies, and on the people who sustain them as they are. To bring about righteousness means that beyond judgement which shows light on what is death-giving, there is a call to reorientate ourselves towards what is life-giving. In order to do this, immense change may be required.

Currently, our planet is dying. The world that God created, beautiful, lush, carefully crafted with its wealth of ecosystems and biodiversity, is overheating, polluted, overrun by plastics and in danger of catastrophic failure. And we know that different communities contribute more than others to this process, and yet it is the communities that produce least pollution that are likely to suffer most.

What do justice and righteousness look like in the face of environmental catastrophe? What judgement would be righteous on the practices and desires that lead to unbridled consumption and the refusal to change our lifestyles for the sake of our fellow humans and the many other life-forms we share the world with? What would justice and righteousness look like in the face of desperate people running away from violence, conflict and poverty, left to die in boats in the Mediterranean because our immensely privileged countries refuse to share their wealth?

These questions relate to huge systems, with multiple moving parts and powerful interests and lobbies. And yet to believe in the Prince of

Peace who brings *shalom* to the whole world is to believe that we are called to model our humanity on the way in which he lived, to believe that it is possible for humanity to live better and love better than it currently does. But to do that, we need to be honest with ourselves about the roots of inequality and injustice in our world. We need to return to the desert.

In the desert, Israel came face-to-face with itself, with God and with the complexity of how to live in the wider world. It would have been easy for Israel, coming out of Egypt, to imagine that all the wrong of the world had come about because of the Egyptians. It would have been easy to blame 'them', the 'others', those with power and lure themselves into believing that they would do better. The story, however, does not go in that direction. Even in Egypt, we meet those who are willing to risk their status and lives on behalf of the Hebrews, such as Pharaoh's daughter. When the people go into the desert, they are called to learn a different way of living: being content with having enough bread for today (manna), taking time out of production and productivity for the sabbath, learning not to compete for food and not to hoard for themselves. Again and again, they are told, 'Remember that you were a slave', and, 'you were aliens' (e.g. Exodus 22:21; 23:9; Leviticus 19:34; Deuteronomy 5:15; 15:15; 16:12). Israel is not immune to the disease of Egypt; their hearts are just as easily corrupted by the desire for wealth and power, over and against an 'other' they despise, use or exploit.

To do justice, in the story of Israel, is to learn to think in a completely different way, to step completely out of the existing system and learn from the God who is outside our broken human ways of thinking and relating, so that something new, strange and disruptive can take root and replace competition, othering and seeking justice through violence and force. It is not something human beings find easy. Ultimately, it isn't something they can learn simply through the law and the word of God. It is something that needs to be embodied and shown – in Jesus Christ. Jesus embraces humanity, and in this embrace transforms them all. He brings about justice and righteousness, not through the sword, but through the cross.

For reflection

- Today, spend some time praying through the news, at home and abroad, and asking God to help you see what justice and righteousness might say in response to even the smallest items.

God of justice and righteousness,
help us enlarge our minds,
that we might take in those we fail to consider;
enlarge our minds,
that we might listen to advice and wisdom we often ignore;
enlarge our hearts,
that we may be willing to share more generously,
and welcome those who differ from us
through culture, practice and beliefs.
Enlarge our hearts,
that we may refuse to reject the other,
however objectionable we may find them.
Enlarge our imagination,
that we may build a different world,
one we cannot quite glimpse,
but that you yourself already hold
in the palm of your hand.
Amen.

DAY 24

Forevermore

For a child has been born for us,
    a son given to us;
authority rests upon his shoulders,
    and he is named
Wonderful Counsellor, Mighty God,
    Everlasting Father, Prince of Peace.
Great will be his authority,
    and there shall be endless peace
for the throne of David and his kingdom.
    He will establish and uphold it
with justice and with righteousness
    from this time onwards and forevermore.

ISAIAH 9:6–7

Today, on Christmas Eve, time stretches out in all directions. It stretches back: to this point in history when the Christ child was fully revealed, after nine months of growing hidden presence; further back to Isaiah and veiled promises; and throughout the history of the people of God, when promise after promise was made of God's presence and deliverance. Time stretches sideways, encompassing in the promise those who were not there physically, but are beloved by a God reaching out to them anyway. And time stretches forward, through history, this one night remembered year after year until today, and forward into tomorrow and a promised future we can only glimpse.

To be human is to be finite, time-limited, fragile – and yet, in the promise of Jesus Christ, we touch something beyond ourselves, the promise of life beyond our finitude. It is only a glimpse, however. The promise is there: our humanity will remain, yet be transformed; we will still be bodily creatures, but bodies will no longer decay; we will still be social and relational, but without the jagged edges of brokenness that cause us to hurt one another; we will still live and love, yet do so in ways that yield flourishing for all – including ourselves. It is a future we cannot quite imagine, because it is so different from our present. And yet it is the future held in the words of Isaiah above.

It is a promise, and like all promises it is fragile, subject to interpretation, and only as good as the one who makes it. Fortunately, it is God who makes the promise. We are secure in the knowledge that God is the guarantor of the future that we glimpse. Yet, just like the people of God throughout history, holding the promise still hurts in a world that seems to negate everything that is being promised. Abraham – a man of faith, beloved, who received a promise (more than once) – still got tired of waiting and doubted, not necessarily what God had said but what he had heard. 'Has God really said…?' are words human beings may utter again and again, sometimes combatively, sometimes tentatively, sometimes full of self-doubt. Abraham had been promised life, a son, but Sarah was too old to bear children, and the promise of life was threatened by the reality of finitude and death. So Abraham tried to make the promise happen by other ways and had a son with Hagar, Sarah's servant. This was a son who received a promise, but not the son of the initial promise.

It is easy to wonder why Abraham doubted, looking at the story retrospectively. God appeared to him multiple times; God spoke to him in prayer; God did give him the promised son and another son by Hagar. Yet in the midst of it, Abraham was lost in the time of waiting. God did appear, but God's words were few and far between in the landscape of an entire life. God's promise did materialise, but it did so late in life, against the odds and with only one precious, fragile child. As years of waiting stretch out, it is easy to lose sight of the promise and concentrate instead on signs of limitation, death and threat around us.

The story of Christ is also one of promise under threat. From a child born in precarious circumstances to death on a cross, it must have looked like a strange fulfilment of a long-ago promise to those looking on, hoping and waiting. The life of Christ spoke of promise fulfilled, but his death threatened everything the disciples would have expected, despite Jesus' own warnings. Life in the world is poised in this moment between life and death, presence and absence, promise and failure. To be human is to be asked to have faith – to trust in the promise in the face of everything that negates it and to live a life that does not fit with what seems to be the reality of the world around. To be human and to follow Christ is to live in a world governed by a different imagination, a different time, a different way.

The promise is not just wishful thinking, however. It is not blind trust. The promise is anchored in memory, in the story we remember of God at work over time – 'Lord, for the years', as the title of the hymn goes. To nurture life in the promise means to nurture and keep alive the memory of God at work, in the pages of scripture and the pages of history – of our churches, our communities and our individual lives. We need to be people who tell stories – to one another, to ourselves, to our children, so that when the shadows close in and rumours of God seem to fade, we keep alive our knowledge of God-among-us, and together with it, our ability to recognise God when God comes slowly, silently and in unexpected places.

For reflection

- What stories would you want to tell of God at work in your own life and the lives of others around you? How can these stories help you shape your walk with God?

God of memory and promise,
the God of Abraham, Isaac and Jacob,
and God of today, tomorrow and forever,
on this night we thank you
for the gift of the Christ child,
for the gift of the life of Christ, his death and resurrection,
and the continued life that you share with us.
Help us approach the crib
with renewed wonder and thankfulness
that you hold time in your hands,
and our destinies
are hidden in Christ with you,
safely and gently
anchored in the memory of your action
and secure in your promise of redemption.
Amen.

CHRISTMAS DAY

Born among us

Joseph also went from the town of Nazareth in Galilee to Judea, to the city of David called Bethlehem, because he was descended from the house and family of David. He went to be registered with Mary, to whom he was engaged and who was expecting a child. While they were there, the time came for her to deliver her child. And she gave birth to her firstborn son and wrapped him in bands of cloth and laid him in a manger, because there was no place in the guest room.

LUKE 2:4–7

Christmas Day dawns, and the long wait is over. The child is born. I wonder what it must have been like for God in human form to move from humanity constrained in the womb to humanity held in the arms of a mother. What must it have been like for the one who is God to have a first embodied taste of hunger? First food? For those small fists to touch new textures – Joseph's beard, Mary's face? To open eyes for the first time and see indistinct shapes, trying to make sense of them with human eyes?

That God, who is beyond everything, above everything, who knew everything, chose to shrink to these human proportions is astonishing. And yet – God's embrace of humanity opens up new and uncharted waters. The God who had made space for another, for the world, for human beings, to 'be', is now entering the space he had created, on the very terms he created it. With the same constraints, the same joys, the same pain, the same risks. God made flesh.

And in face of the immensity of what happens at Christmas, it is easy for us to concentrate on the extraordinary and somehow, slowly but surely, divorce Christmas from its earthy, grounded reality. The challenge of Christmas is to hold the extraordinary and the ordinary together in one breath and refuse to separate them. It is easy to turn Christmas into an event that tells us mostly, or only, about God. But Christmas also tells us about ourselves: the kind of worlds we construct for a child to come into; the kind of people we are, dependent on one another for survival. It tells us about our bodily existence, our dependence on earth's bounty and on the bodies and kindness of others. It speaks of our fragility, and, beyond anything, of our belovedness.

I often wince slightly at the words of a popular Christmas carol. In 'O come, all ye faithful', we sing, 'Lo, he abhors not the virgin's womb.' I am sure the intent is a good one. But it sounds as if a womb is something slightly repellent that God had to endure with gritted teeth. And at one level – of course. That 'God of God, Light of Light' should be made flesh in this manner is incomprehensible. But incomprehensible does not mean it should be a reason to 'abhor'. The message of Christmas is rather the opposite – that human beings and their bodies are so precious, so beloved, that God chooses to enter their reality to transform it so that human beings can know fullness of life.

The womb in the Bible is not something to ignore or avoid talking about. It is not the subject of embarrassed giggles or awkward silences. The womb is a symbol of life. In Hebrew, it is also the root word for compassion – one of the most celebrated attributes of God. God loves like a mother loves a child – with passion rooted deep inside her, the passion of one who has carried a child within her. At Christmas, there is an odd reversal of roles – God, who is creator, who engendered the world, gave birth to humanity, is now being given birth to by a young woman; God, who loves with the compassion of a mother, is enclosed in the womb and loved with the passion of Mary, the mother of Jesus.

The Word made flesh is not word only, but now enmeshed with the most intimate realities of being human.

We cannot dis-incarnate Christmas. Christmas is about flesh, about the messy reality of birth and of human relations. New life is at work, and new life, as always, is messy. On Christmas Day, the child is born, probably not in a stable as we often picture it, but in the main family room of an ancient dwelling. Ancient houses in Palestine often had an upper room, used as a guest room, but there was no space there for Mary and Joseph, so they stayed in the main family room, where families often brought in their animals at night and where work would have been done. It would have been busy and noisy, full of human – and animal – life. Jesus probably did not arrive in the middle of an ethereal 'silent night', but in the midst of the hustle and bustle of human families and their activities. Jesus was born among us – right in the middle of human normality, of human work, life, sleep, family. New life came unbidden, and its extraordinariness was hidden in the midst of our humanity.

And maybe… maybe it is worth pausing, and thinking about how extraordinary it is to be human, too. How extraordinary the gift of life is. We live on the only inhabitable planet in a gigantic star system. We are surrounded by an immensity largely inimical to life. And yet, on this planet, this gift from God – life – can thrive, and we can live and love and grow. And the creator of this immense universe cares about his small, fragile creatures. What does that say about our humanity? And what does it say about how much we should cherish one another and respect the life among us and between us? If God's creatures are worth so much that he embraced their humanity in every way, then how much more should we hold one another as precious gifts from God?

Christmas is a call to embrace life – the life of the world as we know it and the new life that takes root through Jesus Christ, because both are gifts from the God who loves us. And embracing life means embracing our humanity, in its frailty and its beauty, in its unity and diversity. Because humanity, however broken or limited, is a gift from the God who loves his creatures to such a degree that he came to meet them on their terms – the Word become flesh.

Child in the manger,
God of God, light of light,
immensity made small
to fit our humanity,
yet so much more,
we welcome you in our midst,
we embrace your gift
and open ourselves
to let you embrace us
with the power, love and challenge
of all your divinity.
Amen.

Suggestions for group study

Here are some suggestions for group conversation. There are more questions than may be needed and some are more personal than others. Group facilitators can gauge which questions may be most suitable for their group, then adapt or rephrase them for use in ways that make sense and work in their context. They may also want to use the prayers from the different sections to pray with the whole group.

1 The Word became flesh

This first section explored the meaning of 'becoming flesh', the impact of God taking this unthinkable, extraordinary step towards humanity.

1 In what ways do you think God becoming flesh helps us understand what it means to be human? In what ways does it challenge us?

2 Being flesh makes us deeply connected to other human beings, who share parts of our DNA, who care for our needs or whose needs we care for, who we depend on for our daily living – for food, water, sanitation, etc. How could we help this interconnectedness to be better seen and appreciated in a society that often hides it or resents it?

3 Being flesh is essentially to be fragile and vulnerable. At what time in your life have you felt fragile or vulnerable? How has that made you feel? How do you respond to the fragility of others? What scripture passages do you turn to at times of vulnerability?

4 Much that we aspire to or praise in our society is about pushing beyond limits, about doing more, better or bigger. How has this ethos affected you personally? Has it affected the life of your church at all? How do we, as communities of Christians, discern where to push beyond limits and when to accept and cherish our creatureliness?

5 One of the most famous quotes of Mother Teresa is this: 'There is much suffering in the world – physical, material, mental. The suffering of some can be blamed on the greed of others. The material and physical suffering is suffering from hunger, from homelessness, from all kinds of diseases. But the greatest suffering is being lonely, feeling unloved, having no one. I have come more and more to realise that it is being unwanted that is the worst disease that any human being can ever experience.' How do you, as individuals and as a church, seek to enable every person around you to know that they are profoundly loved by God?

Prayer activity
Being flesh is about being connected. Who are the people you depend on every day, and how? Spend time praying for the people you may not see or know by name and yet are connected to.

2 He came into the world

This section explores how being in the world comes with specific configurations of places and cultures, in the midst of political systems and the reality of conflict and injustice. You may want to explore how life with Christ interacts with this at both local and global levels.

1 The people we meet at the beginning of the gospel all had expectations about God and how God might act in the world and towards them. What are your expectations of God and of life, and where do you think they come from? What are your expectations as a church?

2   Read the Magnificat together. What feelings does it evoke? How might it shape our personal conduct? How does it challenge our ways of life? How is it relevant today?

3   The desert symbolises a time of being shaped and reshaped in the story of the people of God and a time of testing in the life of Jesus. But being reshaped comes with specific practices – like the sabbath and the law given to the people. What practices shape your life together as a church? What about your lives as individuals? (Think: prayer, Bible study, Holy Communion, giving, sung worship, etc.) What do you find helpful or less helpful, and why?

4   The story of Jesus' presentation at the temple gathers together three generations and unites them before God. What times and spaces enable you to practise faith together across generations? How easy is it? What are the challenges? What are the benefits of it? Could you imagine new or different ways to do this?

5   What do you think a 'Christian life in the world' looks like? What would be its defining characteristics? How can churches support their members in living in this way?

Prayer activity
Think about your local area together. Who might be invisible there? How do you reach out to those who struggle? Who might need to be welcomed? Spend some time praying for projects that care for the vulnerable or marginalised.

3 Living the story

This section explores how all of us are part of multiple stories – in our families, our communities, our churches, our nations – and how these relate to the Christian story. This session would be a good one to focus on telling stories.

1 Invite different people to share their story of faith – how they might have come to faith or grown in faith.

2 Where have you seen God at work in your life and in the life of this church? Where has God been at work in the last week? Where has God seemed absent? How do you tell that story too?

3 Who has been really important to you in your journey of faith? Spend time sharing what seems characteristic of those who shape our story, then giving thanks for them in prayer.

4 Which parts of the story or journey have been difficult – particularly as a church or in interaction with church? Can this be placed before God, without attempting to resolve it or explain it away?

5 Which parts of the story of your church or your community never get told? Why do you think that is? How could this be changed – or redeemed?

Prayer activity
After you share stories of your church and your local community, pray for your church and for your local community together, paying attention to those who often get left out.

4 Embodying the promise

Our final section ponders the wonderful promise of Isaiah 9:6–7 and what this might mean for the ways in which God works among us.

1 Much of scripture addresses the question of wisdom and who shapes how we gain wisdom. What is the best bit of wisdom – Christian or not – that you have ever been given or that you have learnt? What makes it wise? How does it fit with the gospel?

2   Isaiah gets right to the heart of our longings and contradictions as human beings – the thirst for power and the fear of power, the longing for peace and the reality of war. What situations in the wider world today inspire you to think about power and might on the one hand, and the need for peace and compassion on the other? Spend some time praying for different parts of the world, while being alert to our human tendency to want 'easy' solutions.

3   Isaiah gives us lots of different ways to think about God, which is good, because God can never be reduced to one concept or image. What kind of feelings and thoughts does each one evoke in you? What images of God more generally do you find most helpful and why? What do you find unhelpful?

4   How might the words of Isaiah help you pray for peace for your own community, nation and the wider world?

5   Isaiah speaks of power and might and of authority. None of these words are very comfortable today, given what we know of abuses of all of these, and yet they are realities of our world. Spend some time thinking about the different types of power all of us have in our lives: over ourselves and others; in terms of things we have access to; in terms of stories we tell. How can we each recognise the power we do have and use it well? Where do we feel powerless – and how do we inhabit that too?

6   As you come to the end of this Advent journey, spend some time considering what promises the story of Christmas makes, and how you might hold on to these in the months to come.

Prayer activity
Think of places in the world where peace is elusive and people in the world who experience injustice and suffering. Spend time praying together for all these places and people. As you pray, keep returning to Isaiah's promise and finish by re-reading Isaiah 9.

Notes

1   Jim Cotter, *Prayer at Night: A book for the darkness* (Cairns Publications, 2014).
2   **who.int/news-room/fact-sheets/detail/levels-and-trends-in-child-mortality-report-2021**
3   James Truslow Adams, *The Epic of America* (Transaction publishers, 1931), p. xii.
4   Mother Teresa, *A Simple Path* (Ballantine Books, 1995).
5   Henri Nouwen, *You Are The Beloved: Daily meditations for spiritual living*, compiled and edited by G. Earnshaw (Hodder and Stoughton, 2018).
6   Friedrich Nietzsche, *Beyond Good and Evil* (reissue edition, Penguin, 2003).

Christmas is a musical destination as well as a spiritual one, yet when we reach the newborn Christ child in the manger, what do we see? What music do we hear in our hearts as we join our songs with those of the angels? In 25 short chapters, each concluding with a specially written prayer, Gordon Giles explores the spiritual and biblical allusions to be found within our best-loved Christmas carols. *A Calendar of Carols* can be used either as an Advent calendar up to Christmas, or more flexibly over the Christmas season and into January.

A Calendar of Carols
Christmas reflections, prayers and songs of praise
Gordon Giles
978 1 80039 279 3 £9.99

brfonline.org.uk

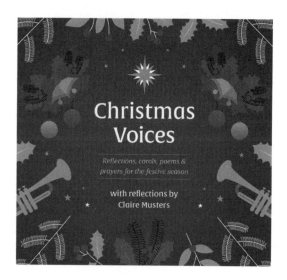

25 short reflective pieces for the Christmas season written by Claire Musters, travelling through promise and preparation to joy, peace and finally love. Along the way we encounter a choir of diverse voices sharing their favourite carols, poems and prayers, illustrated throughout with original colour artwork. Includes contributions from Mags Duggan, Gordon Giles, Isabelle Hamley, Chine McDonald, Lucy Moore and many more.

Christmas Voices
Reflections, carols, poems and prayers for the festive season
Claire Musters
978 1 80039 230 4 £9.99

brfonline.org.uk

Explore the profound meaning of Easter beyond personal spirituality. There is no doubt that each of us has a place in the Easter story, but what happened on the cross is not just a story of me and Jesus. It is far deeper and wider than that. In this Lenten journey, Jo Swinney explores the broader impact of the Easter story on God's relationship with creation. Through Bible readings, reflections and stories from A Rocha International's global conservation efforts, discover how the cross transforms not just our own individual connection with Jesus, but also our relationships with each other and our world.

BRF Lent Book: The Whole Easter Story
Why the cross is good news for all creation
Jo Swinney
978 1 80039 269 4 £9.99

brfonline.org.uk

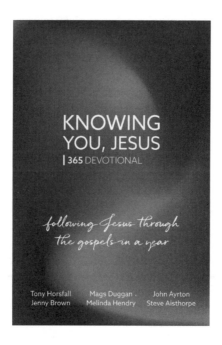

KNOWING
YOU, JESUS
| 365 DEVOTIONAL

following Jesus through
the gospels in a year

Tony Horsfall   Mags Duggan   John Ayrton
Jenny Brown   Melinda Hendry   Steve Aisthorpe

Inspired by the famous prayer of Richard of Chichester 'to see thee more clearly, love thee more dearly and follow thee more nearly... day by day', this 365-day devotional encourages faith formation and intentional discipleship. Tony Horsfall, Mags Duggan, John Ayrton, Jenny Brown, Melinda Hendry and Steve Aisthorpe present a detailed, chronological exploration of the life of Jesus of Nazareth, drawing from all four gospels. As we immerse ourselves in the story, may we not only understand it better but experience transformation into the likeness of Christ our Saviour.

Knowing You, Jesus: 365 Devotional
Following Jesus through the gospels in a year
Tony Horsfall, Mags Duggan, John Ayrton, Jenny Brown, Melinda Hendry and Steve Aisthorpe
978 1 80039 185 7   £19.99

brfonline.org.uk

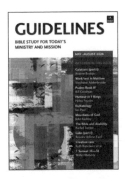

Isabelle Hamley is a contributing author to *Guidelines*, a unique Bible reading resource that offers four months of in-depth study, drawing on the insights of current scholarship. Its intention is to enable all its readers to interpret and apply the biblical text with confidence in today's world, while helping to equip church leaders as they meet the challenges of mission and disciple-building. Instead of the usual dated daily readings, *Guidelines* provides weekly units, broken into six sections, plus an introduction giving context for the passage, and a final section of points for thought and prayer.

Guidelines

Bible study for today's ministry and mission
Edited by Rachel Tranter and Olivia Warburton
Published three times a year in January, May and September

brfonline.org.uk/guidelines

BRF Ministries

Inspiring people of all ages to grow in Christian faith

BRF Ministries is the home of Anna Chaplaincy, Living Faith, Messy Church and Parenting for Faith

As a charity, our work would not be possible without fundraising and gifts in wills.
To find out more and to donate,
visit brf.org.uk/give or call +44 (0)1235 462305